School Of The Prophets

A Curriculum For Success

Kimberly Hargraves

Copyright © 2017 by Kimberly Hargraves.

All rights reserved
Rejoice Essential Publishing
P.O. BOX 85
Bennettsville, SC 29512
www.republishing.org

All rights reserved. No part of this book may be used or reproduced by any means, graphic, electronic, or mechanical, including photocopying, recording, taping or by any information storage retrieval system without the written permission of the publisher except in the case of brief quotations embodied in critical articles and reviews.

Unless otherwise indicated, Scripture is taken from the King James Version.

Scriptures quotation marked EXB are from the Expanded Bible. Copyright © 2011 by Thomas Nelson Inc. Used by permission All rights reserved.

Scriptures quotation marked NASB are from New American Standard Bible Copyright © 1960, 1962, 1963, 1968, 1971, 1972, 1973, 1975, 1977,1995 by THE LOCKMAN FOUNDATION A Corporation Used by permission All Rights Reserved

Scriptures quotation marked NIV are from, New International Version®, Copyright © 1973, 1978, 1984, 2011 by Biblica, Inc.™ Used by permission of Zondervan. All rights reserved.

Visit the author's website at www.kimberlyhargraves.com

While the author has made every effort to provide accurate internet addresses at the time of publication, neither the publisher nor the author assumes any responsibility for errors or for changes that occur after publication.

School Of The Prophets: A Curriculum For Success/Kimberly Hargraves

ISBN-10: 1-946756-08-3
ISBN-13: 978-1-946756-08-4

Library of Congress Control Number: 2017942310

DEDICATION

To my Lord and Savior Jesus Christ. First John 4: 19 (KJV) says, " We love him, because he first loved us." John 3:16 (KJV) says, "For God so loved the world that He gave His only begotten Son, that whosoever believeth in Him should not perish, but have everlasting life." First Peter 3:18 (KJV) says, "For Christ also hath once suffered for sins, the just for the unjust, that He might bring us to God, being put to death in the flesh, but quickened by the Spirit."

Contents

Acknowledgments vii
Foreword viii
Introduction 1
Testimonies 4
Is The School Of The Prophets Biblical? 6
Mentorship 10
What Is Prophecy? 15
Hearing God's Voice 22
Lifestyle Of A Prophet 28
Spirit Of Prophecy 37
Gift Of Prophecy 45
Office Of A Prophet 53
Gifts Of The Spirit 60
Functions Of A Prophet 71
Call Of A Prophet 87
Benefits Of Prophecy 93
Preparation Of A Prophet 98
False Prophets 107
Warfare 118
Curriculum 123

ACKNOWLEDGMENTS

THANK YOU TO EVERYONE WHO SUPPORTS THIS MINISTRY. I AM SO EXCITED ABOUT WHAT GOD IS DOING. HE HAS AMAZING PLANS FOR EACH AND EVERY ONE OF US. I AM SO GLAD THAT YOU DECIDED TO INVEST IN YOURSELF SPIRITUALLY. GET READY TO GO HIGHER IN GOD.

Foreword

If you are called to be a prophet or prophetess then this is the book for you. Prophetess Kim does an awesome job at breaking down the dimensions of the prophetic. She helps us understand the gift of prophecy and the office of a prophet. She shows us how the LORD use prophets not only to speak but to perform miracles. I look for two things when I read most books, scriptures and testimonies. I want to see what you're saying in the word and in your life. And she did just that. She gave us a glimpse into her life and her relationship with God. I've read numerous books on this subject and this is definitely one of my favorites. I love how she incorporates prayer, fasting and a lifestyle of worship. And not only that, but a prophet should have a lot of word in them. Prophet's not only confirm but they can also deliver new revelation from God. People are saying all you need a prophet to do is confirm what God already said to you. That's a lie from the pits of hell. It's a doctrine of devils.

It's the enemy's way of getting you to shut down new revelation from the LORD, because he knows the first thing the people of God will say is "God didn't tell me that." But this book is not about giving people a word and speaking for God, it's deeper than that. This book is about being God's friend. You need alone time with the LORD on a daily basis to hear His voice. The voice of the LORD is not just "SOUND" His voice is His word. His voice is dreams and visions. His voice is a knowing or an impression. His voice is signs, wonders, and miracles. His voice comes as confirmation that you can see or hear. Before He use you in public, He trains you in private. In the midst of reading the book I found myself yearning for more. Every time I turned the page there was a deeper desire to know Him on a level that I have not known. And to hear Him in ways that I have not heard Him. Whether you're listening to a person preach, teach, or you're reading a book, If it's anointed, it should give you a greater desire for Jesus.

This book is inspired by the Holy Spirit. Believe me, I would never write a foreword for a book I didn't believe in. She has so much revelation about the prophetic to share with you. I would advise the reader not to rush through this book but take your time. Read it, go pray, study the word, then come back for more. My friend, you are about to embark on a deeper level of intimacy with the father. If you are reading this it's not an accident, you didn't just stumble across this book, but God is calling you higher. Your worship, your prayer life and your prophetic flow is about to tap into new realms. This book will give you so much information and revelation, but you still need to learn how He speaks to you. The bible says, "A wise man will hear and increase learning" (Proverbs 1:5). I know this book will bless you tremendously, because it blessed me.

Tron Moses, Founder and CEO of Tron Moses' Photography

CHAPTER ONE

Introduction

Welcome to the School of the Prophets: A Curriculum For Success. This book is inspired by the Holy Spirit as a gift to the body of Christ. I have been graced to write and to instruct. 1 Peter 4:10 says, "As every man hath received the gift, even so minister the same one to another, as good stewards of the manifold grace of God." I want people to be able to take this teaching back to their communities, churches, home bible studies, etc. and to be able to teach from it. At the end of this book is a curriculum, and throughout the book are mini assignments which consists of questions to ensure that one is retaining the material being taught. There are also prophetic exercise throughout this book. Take the time and seek God. When you place yourself in a posture to receive from God you will be amazed at the revelation you will receive. These exercises will help you grow and to sharpen your spiritual gifts.

Teacher's notes

I highly recommend that the instructor fasts and worships before each class. It is vital that you have a have a prophetic anointing. You want to bring the spirit of the Lord with you to class. The reason is to ensure that the spirit of prophecy is present so that the students are able to prophesy with ease. Make sure you thoroughly study the lessons before teaching a class. 2 Timothy 3:16 says "All scripture is given by inspiration of God, and is profitable for doctrine, for reproof, for correction, for instruction in righteousness." This book will provide sound doctrine for training others in the prophetic and cultivating a prophetic lifestyle. God will bless your sacrifice for training others.

Student notes

I encourage each student to not give up when faced with a challenge. The only way to grow spiritually at times is to be stretched and to be out of your comfort zone. I encourage you to have your mind made-up to finish what you have started. Make a decision that quitting is not an option, no matter how difficult the tasks may seem. Come to each class hungry for the things of the spirit and put forth a great effort. You will be amazed at the results. The teaching inside this book is based off the word of God and it is designed for you to go back and forth to the bible.

Self-Taught

Maybe you don't plan on teaching a class to others, but just want to learn about the prophetic. Great! This book is still for you. That's the versatility of this book, it's for everyone who just wants to know more and to learn. Make sure you have a composite book present so you can complete the assignments at the end of the chapter. You don't want to rob yourself of the fullest that this book has to offer you. 2 Timothy 2:15 says, "Study to shew thyself approved unto God, a workman that needeth not to be ashamed, rightly dividing the word of truth."

CHAPTER TWO

Testimonies

These are the testimonies taken from my website about the school of the prophets. The names of the students have been abbreviated to respect their privacy. Hopefully these testimonies will inspire you to learn and show you that God is doing something great here with this school. Revelation 12:11 says, "And they overcame him by the blood of the Lamb, and by the word of their testimony; and they loved not their lives unto the death."

I feel like I have grown. I'm building my confidence to just trust God and speak. This course was great (M Amber)

I do feel like I grew in my gift it made me more confident in what I was hearing... I really enjoyed myself at the same time even though I was nervous. This class it is very fun... it opens a door for you to start doing what God called you to (SBlue).

I feel like I've grown in my gift (MMason).

Thank you for this course. It has been awesome and I have been honored. I do feel like I have grown indeed. Before I was not as keen at seeing but now I'm a bit more confident (SMcClendon).

Having the ability to have someone confirm or respond right away. As my faith trembled, it was renewed and strengthened with every confirmation (KGeorge).

Prophetess I feel like I have grown soooooooo much in just a matter of 3 or 4 weeks. This was awesome. I wished it was a lil longer (BMcClendon).

I would recommend the class to others. Prophetess Kimberly is a great teacher and the anointing she carries is awesome. (TNcho)

I enjoyed learning about the Prophetic Office and prophesy. I was stretched by the assignments, and how each assignment showed me things about myself (TCampbell).

Interaction with the class and watching everyone evolve under one of the greatest teacher ever Prophetess Kimberly Hargraves (EAlbritton).

CHAPTER THREE

Is the School of The Prophets Biblical?

I hear so many people say, "No one can teach you how to prophesy or to become a prophet." I tell people that I train them to be confident in hearing God for themselves so they don't have to always seek a prophet. I also tell them that I will teach them to flow with the Holy Spirit. When I first got called to be a prophet, I heard God but I didn't know how to flow with the Holy Spirit. My mind was full of doubt and I was full of fear. I didn't understand the gifts of the spirit and was very unsure about stepping out and allowing the Lord to use me. All the worries faded away when I attended a prophetic boot camp. This training changed my life and I learned how to flow with the Holy Spirit.

The people who oppose prophecy probably will never prophesy because there has to be a desire for it (1 Corinthians 14:1). There has to be some type of training to sharpen the gifts that God has placed inside of each of us. Practice makes perfect. For instance, a runner training for the Olympics is constantly exercising and doing drills to increase their speed, sharpen their skill, and prepare them for the big day. The same concept applies to gifts of the spirit. You may be anointed but lack wisdom and not be fully aware of certain things. This is why the Lord placed the five-fold offices in the body of Christ (Ephesians 4:8-12). This is also why mentorship is important and we will discuss that in a later chapter. People have risen up and spoke out against the prophetic movement that is happening in the body of Christ. I have even heard people say, "The school of the prophet isn't biblical." This is not true. This chapter will prove that statement to be false.

In 1 Samuel 19:18–24, King Saul had an evil spirit and he wanted to kill David. David fled several times and went to the prophet Samuel and told him what was going on. Three different times, Saul sent messengers to find David but they all prophesied when they encountered a group, school, or company of prophets that were appointed by Samuel. Saul finally got up and was going to go kill David himself but he prophesied day and night when he encountered these prophets. The prophets in this group were being sharpened by being around each other. Proverbs 27:17 says, "Iron sharpeneth iron; so a man sharpeneth the countenance of his friend." 1 Samuel 19:20 states that these prophets were appointed by Samuel. Samuel was training these prophets. He could've been a spiritual father to these prophets or a mentor. Remember a school of the prophets is bigger than your gift; it's about a lifestyle, character development, the dos and don'ts of ministry, and more. Imagine being new to the prophetic. You might have so many questions and want God to send you a mentor with some experience who has been there and done that.

Think about fishes for a moment. The correct term to call a group of fish together is a school of fish. Fish swim together for social reasons. Prophets are attracted to other prophets and it's quite common for a group of them to stick together. 1 Corinthians 14:32 says, "And the spirits of the prophets are subject to the prophets." Let's look at some more biblical ways prophets grouped together. In several places in scripture there is a term called "sons of the prophets." We will look through some of these examples to gain a greater understanding. In 2 Kings 2, we read the story of Elijah being taken to heaven. In four different verses (2 Kings 2:3,5,7,15) in this chapter we see the same term, "sons of the prophets." The sons of the prophets means a group, brotherhood, company, or school of the prophets. Elisha met some sons of the prophets in Bethel then in Jericho. They even searched for Elijah for three days after he was taken away but was unable to find him.

In 2 Kings 4, there are several verses that mention the sons of the prophets. Now we see the prophet Elisha operating in a different role. He is no longer the protegee, but a mentor to many prophets. Elisha believed in mentorship because he was under Elijah for years way before he did any ministry. The sons of the prophets are mentioned again in 2 Kings 4:1,38, 2 Kings

5:22, 2 Kings 6:1-2, 2 Kings 9:1, 1 Kings 20:35, Amos 7:14, and Acts 3:25. You can now see that throughout scripture that there has always been a group, company, or school of the prophets. Don't be one of those people who claim to be a prophet but can't even prophesy. Get some training by attending the school of the prophets.

Quick Review:

1) Is the school of the prophets biblical?

2) Why are prophets attracted to one another?

3) What are some places in the bible where the school of the prophets can be found?

4) Critical Thinking Question: Have you found your prophetic company?

CHAPTER FOUR

Mentorship

Mentorship is so vital to the body of Christ. Think of the word mentorship as discipleship. We can see that plainly happening in certain scriptures throughout the bible. The main reason for a mentor is to get training, advice, and impartation before walking in destiny and purpose. Even when you are already walking in purpose, honoring your mentors is still important. In today's society, many people don't want to learn and be taught; instead they are in a rush. They end up making countless mistakes that could have been avoided if they were accountable to someone and took the time to be developed. Luke 6:40 says, "The disciple is not above his master: but every one that is perfect shall be as his master."

Many people are lost and just searching for answers. Mentors can help bring clarity and direction to people who are babes in the gospel. Part of the fivefold offices is to train and equip the body of Christ (Ephesian 4:11-12). We can see so many people who claim to be in one of these offices failing because they aren't completing their tasks. One of the qualities of a great leader is to raise up the next generation and not be intimidated by the anointing on their lives. A great leader will want their spiritual sons and daughters to do greater works and more than they have ever done. Let's look at what Jesus said because he is the ultimate example of our faith. John 14:12 says, "Verily, verily, I say unto you, He that believeth on me, the works that I do shall he do also; and greater works than these shall he do; because I go unto my Father."

You have failed as a leader if you weren't able to duplicate the anointing on your life in your protégées, impart into the next generation, and you are the only one operating in signs and wonders but nobody else around you is. I have seen so many leaders who were jealous of the people who attended their churches or were underneath them to learn. It makes me proud to impart into someone who has never operated in healing, deliverance, or prophesied before. So many people have attended my training and they are flowing better than me and I praise God for that. I am not jealous of them but I encourage and push them to reach their fullest potential in Christ Jesus. At the end of the day, God imparts unto a stronger grace and anointing to me because the more I give, the more I receive.

Now, we are all called to disciple someone. You don't have to have a title or be behind a pulpit. We are all a leader in our own right. Someone out there looks up to you in some form or fashion. You may say, "How can I possibly disciple someone?" Well it starts by getting training yourself and learning the word. Then you are able to teach someone else everything that you know. Did you know that mentoring/discipling is a mandate or a command? It's part of the great commission. If you say you believe in Christ then you are called to mentor and to spread the gospel. Matthew 28:19-20 says, "Go ye therefore, and teach (disciple/mentor) all nations, baptizing them in the name of the Father, and of the Son, and of the Holy Ghost: Teaching them to observe all things whatsoever I have commanded you: and, lo, I am with you always, even unto the end of the world. Amen."

Let's look at some examples of mentorship in the bible. Let's start with Jesus. He mentored his disciples in Luke 9. He told his disciples to imitate him (1 Corinthians 11:1). He suffered and left his disciples an example to follow (1 Peter 2:21). He told his disciple if they didn't take up their cross, carry their cross, and follow after him then they weren't worthy of him (Matthew 10:38, Luke 14:27). He told his disciples in Matthew 11:29 to take is yoke and learn from him. He told his disciples in Matthew 4:19 that he would make them fishers of men. Lastly, he told his disciples that they would be witnesses of him and that they shall receive power when the Holy Spirit came upon them (Acts 1:8).

Moses was mentored by his father in law Jethro. Let's read Exodus 18. Moses sat around from morning till evening every day judging the people. Can you imagine working like this every day? What kind of social life would you have? How could you have time to spend with family or friends? How could you spend time with God? Jethro gave Moses advice and told him what he was doing is not good because he would wear himself out. He told him to raise up able men, and Moses listened and did everything he was advised. Now, this is the benefit of having a mentor. A mentor is able to see the positives and the negatives. A mentor is able to provide sound advice to make your ministry more effective.

Eli mentored young Samuel in the first four chapters of 1 Samuel. Samuel was able to look at the life of Eli and recognize the dos and don'ts of ministry. He was able to learn about God and the ways of the temple from Eli. Now, I was able to learn about the dos and don'ts of ministry as well when I was being mentored. This is why I am so passionate about mentoring others, because I want people to have someone that believes in them and launches them forward when they have proven themselves to be ready. Another example of mentorship is when Apostle Paul encourages his spiritual son Timothy to stir up the spiritual gifts within him. 2 Timothy 1:6 says, "Wherefore I put thee in remembrance that thou stir up the gift of God, which is in thee by the putting on of my hands." Apostle Paul was a great mentor because he imparted into his spiritual son and wanted him to use his spiritual gifts not hinder him from flowing with God. Apostle Paul wanted Timothy to reach his fullest potential in God, he wasn't jealous that he could be flowing in a greater dimension than him. When students take my courses, I am mentoring them.

Quick Review:

1)   What is mentorship?

2) Provide some biblical examples of mentorship.

3) What ways do leaders fail the next generation?

4) Critical Thinking Question: Have you ever been mentored and what were your experiences?

CHAPTER FIVE

What is Prophecy?

A lot of people get prophets confused with psychics. This is what I thought when I first heard of the prophetic. I remember praying to God about marriage restoration. I was broken and obsessed with praying for marriages that were broken. I would spend hours praying every prayer I could get my hands on pertaining to marriage restoration. I looked up every scripture about marriage and decreed them. One day as I was praying, I heard the Lord speak to me. I heard, "You are a prophet." I thought I was hearing things. So, I ignored it. Then I heard him tell me again that I was a prophet. I just shook it off immediately because I thought there must be a mistake. I thought prophets were only Caucasian obese males with long beards and that I couldn't possibly be a prophet because I didn't look like that. I realize that my mind was racing, so I got up from the spot on the floor where I was praying and walked through my apartment at that time. Again, I heard the Lord speak to me and this time he gave me a bunch of dates. I remember hearing 9, 27, and the other numbers I don't recall. I looked up biblical numerology on a website called Arithmetic of God[1] and there it was! I saw the word prophecy. Twenty-seven means the proclamation of prophecy. Nine means the fruits of the spirit. I was about to fall out on the floor. From that moment, my life has never been the same. The Lord put such a burden upon me that I had no other choice but to speak as his oracle. I made a decision to study and find out everything that I possibly could on the prophetic.

Let's answer the question, "What is prophecy." 1 Corinthians 14:3 (KJV) says, "But he that prophesieth speaketh unto men to edification, and exhortation, and comfort." This verse describes the basic level of prophecy which is edification, exhortation, and comfort. We will break down each word to further help your understanding. Prophecy edifies, which is another word for building. So many are built up through prophecy. Think about how a new believer just doesn't know the standards of the word of God or how someone who has been saved but is on the verge of backsliding. This is where prophecy comes in. The prophetic word could be, "God says return to your first love. I need you to seek me more." This word can be edifying or up-building because it will draw the believer in to seek God, put him first, and cut away the things that are compromising their walk with God. The church is God's building and it is built up through prophecy. Ekklesia is the Greek word for assembly or called out one. This is where the word church comes from[2]. We are the church which is a body of believers. Let's look at an example of where Apostle Paul calls an assembly of believers the church.

Romans 16:5 says, "Likewise greet the church that is in their house. Salute my well-beloved Epaenetus, who is the firstfruits of Achaia unto Christ."

Next let's take a look at the word exhortation. Exhortation is the Greek word paraklesis, which means "solace, entreaty, consolation, admonition or comfort.[3]" This word is related to the word parakletos, or Comforter, a name for the Holy Spirit. The Holy Spirit uses prophecy to comfort believers and to exhort them to holiness, love, worship, praise, prayer, evangelism, humility and giving. There were times where the Lord used me to give a word of exhortation to others. People began to give God praise for the word of the Lord that exhorted them. Acts 15:32 says, "And Judas and Silas, being prophets also themselves, exhorted the brethren with many words, and confirmed them." God used these two prophets, Judas and Silas to encourage the believers to make them stronger. 1 Timothy 4:13 says, "Till I come, give attendance to reading, to exhortation, to doctrine." Apostle Paul wrote this to his spiritual son Timothy. He told him to continue to read scriptures to people, strengthen, and teach them. Reading of the word such as the book of Psalms can exhort a weary believer.

To comfort someone is the last basic level of the prophetic. Comfort is the Greek noun paramuthia, which means "consolation." This is a different type of comfort, and it is especially important for believers who are suffering or struggling in their faith. For instance, having a prophetic word just brings comfort to your soul whenever you are going through a trial and tribulation. It's a comfort, knowing that God cares about you and He will not forsake you. I recall a time when I was so discouraged about the things I was going through. I was going through a divorce, couldn't pay my bills on time, and felt alone because I was about 1600 miles away from my family. I wanted to quit and just die, but the Lord was mindful of me. He sent a prophet to speak into my life. At that moment, I received comfort and the strength to hold on.

True prophecies originate with God and not man. We see a lot of people prophesying from their flesh or their vain imaginations of their heart. These people are lying on God saying, "God said, God said, and God said." Yet God didn't say what they are accusing God of speaking. For instance, a true prophet of God will be more concerned with the spiritual state of a person if they are in sin instead of prophesying that they will get blessed with a million dollars. To reiterate, true prophecy originates with God and not with man. Prophecy is speaking the plans and the will of God. True prophets are more concerned about pleasing God than men. We will discuss false prophets later in this book. Many prophets want to prove their gift and speak when God is not speaking. To have accuracy in the prophetic, we need to be led by the Holy Spirit. We need to be submitted to him and move under the unction of his spirit. 2 Peter 1:21 (KJV) For the prophecy came not in old time by the will of man: but holy men of God spake as they were moved by the Holy Ghost.

1 Corinthians 14:1 says, "Follow after charity, and desire spiritual gifts, but rather that ye may prophesy." It is great to operate in love. I always tell my students that love makes the gifts work. We don't need to prophesy in anger or pride. It is the

love of God that will win the hardest heart over. The reason why I attended and became a faithful member at my current church is because of the love of God radiating from my pastor's pores. There is nothing wrong with desiring spiritual gifts and prophesying. It is the religious people that will talk you out of desiring to operate in the supernatural. They will say to follow after the gift-giver and not the gift. However, God will not condemn you for wanting these spiritual gifts if your heart and motives are right for wanting them. Our motives should be that we want to advance His kingdom and win souls for His glory. Our motives shouldn't be give me more power to enlarge my platform or to make me famous. Our ultimate goal should be to lift up the name of Jesus. Sometimes, there has to be a desire for something for God to give it to you. People that desire something will put to use of what God gives them instead of allowing it to go to waste.

1 Thessalonians 5:20 says, "Despise not prophesyings." So many people reject the prophetic. They are shutting down what God wants to communicate with them. God has used me so many times to prophesy new things into people's lives. Some people received it, and others rejected it. Those people that rejected it came back to me later and said, "Woman of God, I have been receiving the same word you gave me. A few other people have giving me the exact same word." Some said, "Wow. When you prophesied over me, I thought there was no way but that word came to pass." Sometimes the prophecies go over our heads because our thinking is limited or we miss it by human reasoning. We have to be mindful that we serve a big God and He wants to use us or do things in our lives that are beyond our capacity. If we don't understand the prophetic word that we receive, we

should place that word on the shelf because it could be for a later date. We should also pray over that word to get an understanding of it. However, if a word isn't from God, then the Holy Spirit with in us will not bear witness with it. I tell my students that it's great to prophesy and have the presence of the Lord. It's powerful to have the reassurance of the fire of the Holy Spirit to back up what you are prophesying. Some churches are dry and have an outdated move of God because they have shut down the glory. It is the prophetic that can break demonic strongholds and bring in the Glory.

Prophetic Exercise: Go into a quiet place and ask the Lord to give you one word for the month. You may hear increase, favor, obedience, etc. You may even hear a word that you have never heard of before and have to look it up. After you receive your word, meditate on a scripture concerning that area for a week. This will increase your biblical knowledge and increase your prophetic flow.

Quick Review:

1) What is prophecy?

2) Explain basic level prophecy and provide the Greek text.

3) What are the dangers and the effects of despising prophecy?

4) Critical Thinking Question: How important is making sure that the source of the information that you receive in the spirit originates from the Holy Spirit and not another source?

CHAPTER SIX

Hearing God's Voice

A lot of people desire to hear the voice of God. Some people hear God, but are uncertain if it's truly Him or themselves. Some people aren't in a posture to hear from God because they have many distractions. Hearing God on a consistent basis starts with a relationship. For instance, married couples have to speak to each other in order to communicate. They have to spend time with one another in order to get to know each other. They have to put forth an effort in order for the marriage to work. The same principle can be applied with God. We have to put forth time in prayer, fasting, meditation, worship, and living right in order to be sensitive to His voice. God is always speaking, but it takes our ears to be able to recognize his voice. We also have to tune out the other voices in the realm of the spirit such as the voice of the enemy, our thoughts, angelic ministers, conversations, etc.

to make sure that we are on the right frequency in the spirit. We have to practice hearing the voice of God.

John 10:27 says, "My sheep hear my voice, and I know them, and they follow me." Whenever we know God's voice, we will not be lead astray. I tell my students that this is a good verse to quote before practicing hearing God and to pray before prophesying. When I first realized that I was hearing God, I had to bind up the enemy from speaking to me. I had heard the enemy speak to me for five long years. Every day the devil would tell me that I was going to die and that he was going to kill me. I cried out to God and repented for my sins. God delivered me and touched my mind. The spirit of torment had no other choice but to leave. I had to bind up the voice of the enemy to make sure that I was hearing right. Many times, the Holy Spirit rebuked me for me doubting that I was hearing from him. Over time, I became so much confident in hearing God and I just died to myself and allowed the Holy Spirit to flow through me.

Jeremiah 29:12-13 says, "Then shall ye call upon me, and ye shall go and pray unto me, and I will hearken unto you. And ye shall seek me, and find me, when ye shall search for me with all your heart." Hearing the voice of God is a supernatural occurrence. When you call upon Him and go somewhere to pray without any distractions, God will listen unto you. The true essence of prayer is having a conversation with God. This conversation should be two-way. Unfortunately, that is not always the case. I discuss ways to pray effectively in my book, "The Pray More Challenge." Many people have tons of things on their minds when they pray. Instead of releasing the burdens they may be carrying to the Lord, they hold them in. Their minds may be racing with thoughts of what they are going to do later or what they are going to eat, etc. However, we have to discipline ourselves to really seek God and put 100% focus on Him we will be amazed of the revelation that we receive in prayer. God longs to speak to you as much as you speak to Him. There were times in prayer where I wrote down three or more pages of things the Lord spoke to me.

Proverbs 16:3 says, "Commit thy works unto the Lord, and thy thoughts shall be established." As prophets, prophetic people, and people of God, we have to make sure that we are submitted to God. The more time that we spend with God and get in His word, the more our thoughts begin to change. For instance, I used to be very pessimistic but now I am very optimistic. When it looked like I couldn't pay certain bills and expenses, instead of panicking I changed my thought processes. I began to think on the promises of God and meditate on the relevant scriptures. Over time, those scriptures got deeply embedded within my mind and I found the Holy Spirit tell me the same exact scriptures when a subsequent trial arose.

John 10:4-5 says, "And when he putteth forth his own sheep, he goeth before them, and the sheep follow him: for they know his voice. And a stranger will they not follow, but will flee from him: for they know not the voice of strangers." Recognizing the voice of God takes time and practice. I always recommend taking a notebook and pen into prayer as an act of faith. Our faith moves God. When you have your pen and notepad ready, it is almost saying, "I expect God to speak to me." I recommend having a daily time that you set apart to hear from God. It could be 5 pm every day. I meet with God the same time every day. If I don't keep my prayer time, then He comes seeking me. I will feel an overwhelming sense of His presence and His fire. Immediately, I know that God wants my attention and I need to go pray ASAP! When we know God's voice we won't get confused with other voices we may hear. One key to know that you are hearing from God is that He would never tell you something that goes against His word. This is why it is so vital to have a good foundation of the word in you. Whatever you put inside of you will come out because the Holy Spirit will bring all things to remembrance.

Hebrews 5:14 says, "But strong meat belongeth to them that are of full age, even those who by reason of use have their senses exercised to discern both good and evil." As believers, we need take the proper steps to guarantee spiritual growth. We have to make the time to pray, fast, serve, worship, meditate, and study the word. Babes in Christ have lack of discernment because they probably aren't knowledgeable of certain scriptures, or not sure how to pray and fast. Over time, the more things we go through, the more we learn how to activate our faith and pray etc. Our senses will become exercised to discern good and evil. So, when you are in prayer and you hear or see something in the realm of the spirit, you will start paying attention to other details such as the presence in the room; does it line up with scriptures, does it bear witness with your spirit?

1 Kings 19:12 says, "And after the earthquake a fire; but the Lord was not in the fire: and after the fire a still small voice." The Holy Spirit's voice is a still small voice. When the prophet

Elijah was looking for the voice of God, he found it in the less likely place. He needed God and he felt alone. Think about all the times when you felt alone and didn't understand why you were suffering and going through certain things. You can find comfort in hearing from God and listening to the softest voice you may hear in your head. Prophets have to be patient and sometimes wait in God's presence and receive His consul. Sometimes, I would seek God about an issue and would not hear the answer for many weeks later. Talk about patience!

Psalm 5:3 says, "My voice shalt thou hear in the morning, O Lord; in the morning will I direct my prayer unto thee, and will look up." I have found that praying at certain times is very strategic. There are eight watches of the day and each watch means something significant. We shall seek God in the early hours and before we start our busy day. This is a part of building our relationship with God. Why would God tell a stranger his secrets? We need to become friends of God. How would you feel if you haven't heard from your friend? You probably would feel hurt, rejection, upset, or may feel a variety of emotions. God understands. Make a commitment to have a consistent prayer life. Seek the Lord and ask Him what time is best for you to pray.

Prophetic Exercise: Ask the Holy Spirit for one scripture that He wants you to read or meditate on. You may see it in your mind's eye. You may hear it. You may even have an impression or just a knowing. After you have received, apply it. Remember the more you apply and use what God gives you the more you will receive.

Quick Review:

1) What are some scriptures to meditate on to hear the voice of God?

2) How important is developing a relationship with the Holy Spirit?

3) What are some things that confirm that someone is hearing from God versus hearing from the enemy?

4) Critical Thinking Question: What are some things you can do to increase the prophetic in your life?

CHAPTER SEVEN

Lifestyle Of A Prophet

When you are a prophet you can't do what everyone else is doing. This means that you can't watch everything on television and listen to everything on the radio. Just because something is popular or in demand doesn't make it right or that God is pleased with it. It vexes me as a prophet to see other people who proclaim themselves to be a prophet watching shows that are full of homosexuality, sexual immorality, cursing, murder, etc. As a prophet of the most high God, I refuse to put garbage in my body which is the temple of God. I believe whatever you put inside of you will come out. I want to have a pure prophetic flow. As a prophet, there must be a consecrated lifestyle. We have to be set apart for the Glory of God. Prophets are friends of God.

They are concerned about the things that He is concerned with. They carry his heart and sometimes His burdens.

##

Romans 8:14 says, "For as many as are led by the Spirit of God, they are the sons of God." As prophets, we have to be led by God. We can't worry about what people think about us. We can't be led by man. Prophets have to be totally yielded to God's spirit. This means that we must speak when God speaks. This means that we have to be careful not to release a word out of season. When we pray and hear a word, we need to be good stewards over that word. That means that we have to ask the Lord what to do with that word. Whenever we release a word out of season, it can cause damage. The individual may get mad at God and you. They may not be mature enough to receive that word. Everything you hear in prayer is not meant to be release. Sometimes prophets have to die with God's secrets by taking it to the grave with them. I always question people's motives when they are on social media every few minutes releasing prophetic words. Are they trying to build up their platform or advance God's kingdom? When you are truly spending time with God, you don't have time to really post on social media.

Psalm 37:23 says, "The steps of a good man are ordered by the Lord: and he delighteth in his way." As prophets, our steps need to be ordered by the Lord. In addition, God needs to take pleasure in us. Our lifestyles need to be pleasing to God. We can't afford to grieve and vex the Holy Spirit. We have to remember that we don't belong to ourselves. I made a decision years ago to go all the way with God. I had to let people go who were detrimental to my faith. I have learned a lot of wisdom through the trials and the life experiences. No one is worth destiny. No one should get in your way when it comes to your relationship with God. Prophets of God should never compromise. They have to be sold out to God. Even when God gives them instructions outside of their comfort zone, they still obey.

Proverbs 3:5-6 says, "Trust in the Lord with all thine heart; and lean not unto thine own understanding. In all thy ways acknowledge him, and he shall direct thy paths." Prophets have to trust God with their whole hearts and not try to make sense of everything they hear in prayer. They have to live lifestyles of faith and allow His spirit to lead them. There were many things that God spoke to me things that were over my head. I said, "Lord, if it is your will then so be it." I didn't try to figure out how it was going to happen because I didn't want to fall into doubt. Eventually, everything I heard in prayer had manifested right before my eyes. God will get prophets in situations where they have no other choice but to depend on and trust Him

Fasting

Prophets are called to fast. Fasting humbles our souls and keeps us in a place of vulnerability to God's spirit. We see all throughout scriptures where various prophets fasted and even called fasts. We also see the miraculous occur shortly after. Fasting helps prophets hear God more and enhances their spiritual senses. Let's look at Jesus who is our ultimate example. Matthew 21:11 says, "And the multitude said, This is Jesus the prophet of Nazareth of Galilee." Jesus was a prophet and he also was a teacher, pastor, evangelist, and an apostle. Matthew 4:1-2 says, "Then Jesus was led by the Spirit into the wilderness to be tempted by the devil. After fasting forty days and forty nights, He was hungry." Jesus even fasted. He was led by the Holy Spirit to fast. Whenever God leads you to fast, he provides a supernatural grace for you to do it. Fasting is mandatory in the life of a prophet.

John 13:15 says, "For I have given you an example, that ye should do as I have done to you." Jesus even said himself that he has given us an example to follow. Don't be one of those fleshed-out prophets whose stomach is their god. Sacrifice by prayer and fasting and watch God reward you. I didn't receive certain gifts and anointings until I fasted. I noticed that my sensitivity to the presence of God was heightened. One time, I did a three day fast and I was just so broken. I laid in God's presence the whole time. I had to minister on a prayer call shortly after and many miracles occurred. Lumps were dissolving, crooked spines were straightened, and a deaf ear open. That's the power of fasting.

Exodus 34:27-28 says, "Then the LORD said to Moses, "Write down these words, for in accordance with these words I have made a covenant with you and with Israel." So, he was there with the LORD forty days and forty nights; he did not eat bread or drink water. And he wrote on the tablets the words of the covenant, the Ten Commandments." Moses didn't get the revelation and instructions to write the Ten Commandments until he fasted. This writing has been around for centuries, all because of his obedience. Can you imagine how much of an impact your obedience will cause on people in your community, the world, and generations to come?

Holiness

Prophets need to be holy. There is no compromise. We want our lifestyle to attract God. We want to give his spirit something pure to dwell in. 1 Peter 1:16 says, "Because it is written, Be ye holy; for I am holy." When I first got called, I began to live holy after I got the revelation of what righteousness was. I tell my testimony of my encounter with God in my book, "In Right Standing." God handed me a scepter of righteousness and it changed my life. I was no longer lukewarm but very zealous for God. Then I became a minister of His fire and saw many miracles around me. Afterwards, I saw how much more effective the ministry had become. We have to speak holy conversations because we are the oracles of God. We truly have to close the door to sin.

Ephesians 4:30-32 says, "And do not grieve the Holy Spirit of God, in whom you were sealed for the day of redemption. Get rid of all bitterness, rage and anger, outcry and slander, along with every form of malice. Be kind and tender-hearted to one another, forgiving each other just as in Christ God forgave you." As prophets, we don't want to grieve our best friend, the Holy Spirit. If he is grieved then we should be grieved too. We don't have time for foolishness, but we need to be about our father's business. We have to imitate Christ which means forgiving, walking in love, and blessing our enemies.

Worship

How can you be a prophet and not love to worship? Prophets love worship! I can worship for hours and enjoy every moment of it. Worship attracts God's spirit. It's amazing to feel the fire of God consume me as I enter into worship. Worship can heal a wounded prophet. Many prophets suffer from loneliness and rejection. It's in worship where you receive a breakthrough in your emotions. It's in worship where you receive comfort for your soul. Worship is ministering to the Lord. Worship is loving on God despite what you are going through. The Lord has blessed me numerous times with the provision I needed after long sessions of worship. The Lord has given me a magazine after worship. The Lord has given me ideas for books after I worshipped. Imagine what you can receive from heaven by just worshipping the Father.

Many times, worship bridges the gap to prophecy. The spirit of prophecy will drop after worship. We can see this with the prophet Elisha. 2 Kings 3:15-16 says, "But now bring me a minstrel." And it came about, when the minstrel played, that the hand of the LORD came upon him. He said, "Thus says the LORD, 'Make this valley full of trenches.'" Elisha requested for a minstrel so he could worship. The spirit of prophecy manifested and the prophet was able to give the word of the Lord. Many people get complacent and don't worship. You will find yourself being more accurate in the prophetic after you worship. God will literally fill your mouth and speak even if you aren't trying to prophesy.

Psalm 40:3 says, "And he hath put a new song in my mouth, even praise unto our God: many shall see it, and fear, and shall trust in the Lord." As King David was seeking God, He put a new song in his mouth. Many people will know that God is real and give him praise for how he uses you. I try to worship God for an hour minimum before I minister sometimes, and God just moves. People get healed, delivered, and prophecy comes forth. As a prophet worship is a necessary, not an option.

Commitment

If you are called as a prophet, you have to have a made-up mind. You have to have tenacity. I used to be a Jonah, a runner. I didn't want to do ministry. I didn't want to serve God. However, God led me into the wilderness and I lost everything. I had no other choice but to serve God. I made a firm decision to serve God no matter what I went through. Prophets, you can't give up. The enemy will attack you. As a prophet you will get persecuted, ridiculed, mocked, and so much more. Look at what the prophets went through in the bible. Jeremiah went to prison many times. He was slapped, thrown into a well, threaten, etc. but he still obeyed God no matter how hard it got at times. God was with him and God is with you too.

Romans 12:1-2 says, "Therefore I urge you, brethren, by the mercies of God, to present your bodies a living and holy sacrifice, acceptable to God, which is your spiritual service of worship.

And do not be conformed to this world, but be transformed by the renewing of your mind, so that you may prove what the will of God is, that which is good and acceptable and perfect." As a prophet, we have to present our bodies to God to be used as vessel of honor and Glory unto him. We have to constantly renew our minds on a daily basis so we can stand firm in our faith.

Matthew 5:11-12 says, "Blessed are ye, when men shall revile you, and persecute you, and shall say all manner of evil against you falsely, for my sake. Rejoice, and be exceeding glad: for great is your reward in heaven: for so persecuted they the prophets which were before you." If you decide to live a Godly life, then you will experience much persecution. When I first accepted my call as a prophet, people called me a witch, they walked away, they stabbed me in the back, and they lied on me. I was hurt and broken. Yet, I was able to rejoice because the hand of the Lord lifted me up and did amazing things in my life. At the end of the day, I realized that I am blessed and so are you.

Pray.

As a prophet, it is mandatory to pray. We need to pray without ceasing. How can you be a prophet and not pray? All believers should pray. As a prophet, you are called to intercede. God will show you things before it happens so you can pray about it. God will show you people and give you countries to pray for it. God will warn you in prayer about a situation so you can pray and thwart the plans of the enemy. God has giving me assignments over people that needed prayers. I have seen faces, heard names, and even received words of knowledge about them pertaining their personal lives. I prayed for them and they never knew it.

No matter how much God used Jesus, he always found somewhere to pray. Luke 5:16 says, "And he withdrew himself into the wilderness, and prayed." Jesus was surrounded by many people in the day but at night he had to get alone with God to pray. Luke 6:12 says, "In those days, Jesus went out to the mountain to pray, and He spent the night in prayer to God." A life of a prophet is a lonely one. You can't have everyone in your ear. You have to get in a place to hear from God. Matthew 14:23 says, "After He had sent them away, He went up on the mountain by Himself to pray. When evening came, He was there alone."

Prophetic Exercise: Ask the Holy Spirit for someone on social media who needs intercession and ask for a word for them. Reach out to them and give the word of the Lord. Remember to continue to pray for them.

Quick Review:

1) What does a prophetic lifestyle consist of?

2) What are some ways that the Holy Spirit can be grieved?

3) How important is it to be led by God as a prophet?

4) Critical Thinking Question: What are some ways you can improve your prophetic lifestyle?

CHAPTER EIGHT

Spirit Of Prophecy.

Many people lack clarity about what the spirit of prophecy is. They feel like if they prophesied before than they are a prophet. Yet, that is not true. You have to be proven and tried. God will confirm it and man will affirm it. We will discuss what a prophet is and how they function later in this book. When the spirit a prophecy falls, sinners can prophesy, or animals can prophesy (Numbers 22:28-30). God will use whatever means He has to in order to get His word out. The spirit of prophecy is at the lower end of the dimension of prophecy. When the spirit of prophecy drops, anyone can prophesy just as accurately as someone who is in the office of a prophet. The spirit of prophecy depends on several things which includes if a prophet is there who carries that mantle to create an atmosphere for the prophetic, and an atmosphere of prayer and worship. Let's go on a journey and see the spirit of prophecy in action.

Revelation 19:10 says, "And I fell at his feet to worship him. And he said unto me, See thou do it not: I am thy fellow servant, and of thy brethren that have the testimony of Jesus: worship God: for the testimony of Jesus is the spirit of prophecy." John the revelator wanted to fall down and worship the angel who gave him a message yet the angel said, "The spirit of prophecy is the testimony of Jesus." Whenever we despise prophecy, we are despising the testimony of Jesus. Prophecy consists of God's plans, purposes, and agenda for your life. Why would anyone despise that? You may be going through a test right now but God is speaking and has declared that a testimony will come forth! This is the power of prophecy. To reiterate, the spirit of prophecy is the testimony of Jesus. It's that simple. Let's look at some examples.

Luke 2:25-35 says, "And, behold, there was a man in Jerusalem, whose name was Simeon; and the same man was just and devout, waiting for the consolation of Israel: and the Holy Ghost was upon him. And it was revealed unto him by the Holy Ghost, that he should not see death, before he had seen the Lord's Christ. And he came by the Spirit into the temple: and when the parents brought in the child Jesus, to do for him after the custom of the law, Then took he him up in his arms, and blessed God, and said, Lord, now lettest thou thy servant depart in peace, according to thy word: For mine eyes have seen thy salvation, which thou hast prepared before the face of all people; A light to lighten the Gentiles, and the glory of thy people Israel. And Joseph and his mother marveled at those things which were spoken of him. And Simeon blessed them, and said unto Mary his mother, Behold, this child is set for the fall and rising again of many in Israel; and for a sign which shall be spoken against; (Yea, a sword shall pierce through thy own soul also,) that the thoughts of many hearts may be revealed."

The passages above tell us about a devout man name Simeon. A devout person is someone who is devoted, committed, or loyal to God. He had a relationship with God. He wasn't a prophet, yet the spirit of prophecy came upon him and he prophesied very accurately about the Messiah. He was in the temple where a prophetess named Anna had been fasting, worshipping, and praying day and night (Luke 2:36-38). Prophetess Anna had already set the atmosphere where the spirit of prophecy could be conducive. Simenon walked into the temple and immediately the Holy Spirit quicken his spirit and he knew that the baby that Mary and Joseph were carrying was the Messiah that the Prophets of Old had spoken of. Simeon had never seen Mary or Joseph before that day but when God's spirit came upon him he supernaturally became aware of their identity and God filled his mouth with his words.

Luke 1:67-79 says, "And his father Zacharias was filled with the Holy Ghost, and prophesied, saying, Blessed be the Lord God of Israel; for he hath visited and redeemed his people, And hath raised up an horn of salvation for us in the house of his servant David; As he spake by the mouth of his holy prophets, which have been since the world began: That we should be saved from our enemies, and from the hand of all that hate us; To perform the mercy promised to our fathers, and to remember his holy covenant; The oath which he sware to our father Abraham

,That he would grant unto us, that we being delivered out of the hand of our enemies might serve him without fear, In holiness and righteousness before him, all the days of our life. And thou, child, shalt be called the prophet of the Highest: for thou shalt go before the face of the Lord to prepare his ways; To give knowledge of salvation unto his people by the remission of their sins, Through the tender mercy of our God; whereby the dayspring from on high hath visited us, To give light to them that sit in darkness and in the shadow of death, to guide our feet into the way of peace."

Zacharias wasn't a prophet, but a priest. He was doing his priestly duties in the temple when all of a sudden an angel appeared to him. The angel told him that he and his wife were going to have a baby. Zacharias was in disbelief because his wife and him were old in age. When he began to speak words of doubt, the angel muted him. He wasn't able to speak until his son John the Baptist was born. This is where the spirit of prophecy fell upon him and the Holy Ghost filled him and he prophesied. He prophesied his son's destiny just as accurately as the prophets of old. You don't have to be a prophet to prophesy. If you are a yielded vessel, God can fill you and cause his word to flow from your lips.

1 Samuel 10:1-13 says, "Then Samuel took a vial of oil, and poured it upon his head, and kissed him, and said, Is it not because the Lord hath anointed thee to be captain over his inheritance? When thou art departed from me to day, then thou shalt find two men by Rachel's sepulchre in the border of Benjamin at Zelzah; and they will say unto thee, The asses which

thou wentest to seek are found: and, lo, thy father hath left the care of the asses, and sorroweth for you, saying, What shall I do for my son? Then shalt thou go on forward from thence, and thou shalt come to the plain of Tabor, and there shall meet thee three men going up to God to Bethel, one carrying three kids, and another carrying three loaves of bread, and another carrying a bottle of wine: And they will salute thee, and give thee two loaves of bread; which thou shalt receive of their hands. After that thou shalt come to the hill of God, where is the garrison of the Philistines: and it shall come to pass, when thou art come thither to the city, that thou shalt meet a company of prophets coming down from the high place with a psaltery, and a tabret, and a pipe, and a harp, before them; and they shall prophesy: And the Spirit of the Lord will come upon thee, and thou shalt prophesy with them, and shalt be turned into another man. And let it be, when these signs are come unto thee, that thou do as occasion serve thee; for God is with thee. And thou shalt go down before me to Gilgal; and, behold, I will come down unto thee, to offer burnt offerings, and to sacrifice sacrifices of peace offerings: seven days shalt thou tarry, till I come to thee, and shew thee what thou shalt do. And it was so, that when he had turned his back to go from Samuel, God gave him another heart: and all those signs came to pass that day. And when they came thither to the hill, behold, a company of prophets met him; and the Spirit of God came upon him, and he prophesied among them. And it came to pass, when all that knew him beforetime saw that, behold, he prophesied among the prophets, then the people said one to another, What is this that is come unto the son of Kish? Is Saul also among the prophets? And one of the same place answered and said, But who is their father?

Therefore it became a proverb, Is Saul also among the prophets? And when he had made an end of prophesying, he came to the high place."

The passage above tells the story of young Saul. He was very good-looking and he had sought the prophet Samuel to acquire his father's lost donkeys. After breaking bread with the prophet, Prophet Samuel told Saul where the donkeys were and the things that were going to transpire. Everything that Samuel spoke, it manifested and none of his words fell to the ground. That's one of the signs of a true prophet that we will discuss later in this book. The prophet told Saul that he would prophesy, and he did. I am telling you, the reader of this book, that you will prophesy as well. I am also telling you that you will prophesy on a greater dimension. Saul came across a company of prophets who were worshipping. Be mindful that the prophetic atmosphere was already set. When Saul stepped into this atmosphere, the spirit of prophecy fell upon him that he prophesied. Whenever someone comes into a presence of a prophet, they can prophesy. When I teach my classes, people who have never prophesied before are able to prophesy underneath that prophetic anointing in the atmosphere. They are just flowing but outside of class some students struggle because they aren't prophets. Remember, prophets with that prophetic mantle can create an atmosphere for the spirit of prophecy.

Joel 2:28-29 says, "And it shall come to pass afterward, that I will pour out my spirit upon all flesh; and your sons and your daughters shall prophesy, your old men shall dream dreams, your young men shall see visions: And also upon the servants and upon the handmaids in those days will I pour out my spirit." Whenever God pours out his spirit, the word says we shall prophesy, dream dreams, and see visions. God is no respecter of persons. When we look at these versus spoken by the prophet Joel we can see different classes of socioeconomics and different genders. Sons and daughters symbolizes youth and both sexes. Yes, God can use children to prophesy. Yes, God can use women. Old men and young men means different age brackets. Servant and handmaids means people who are in the lower class of society and people that seem to be over looked. God will use them too.

Prophetic Exercise: Go into worship for about 15 minutes or more and ask the Holy Spirit to show you a vision or a picture of something pertaining to your life. This exercise is to help develop or sharpen your spiritual sight. Once you receive your picture, ask him for the interpretation. You don't want to make assumptions. Some pictures are literal and others are symbolic. Asking for the interpretation is always a good habit to form to make sure you aren't that presumptuous prophet.

Quick Review:

1)   What is the spirit of prophecy?

2)   What some examples of the spirit of prophecy?

3)   Can someone prophecy accurately under the spirit of prophecy? If so, please explain?

4) Critical Thinking Question: How important is creating a prophetic atmosphere? What ways can you develop a prophetic atmosphere in your environment?

CHAPTER NINE

Gift Of Prophecy

The gift of prophecy is different from the spirit of prophecy. It may be years for someone to prophesy again who isn't a prophet when they are in an atmosphere where the spirit of prophecy is present. However, someone with the gift of prophecy prophesies quite frequently because it's a gift from the Holy Spirit. We will discuss the gifts of the Holy Spirit in great detail in another section of this book. Just because someone has the gift of prophecy doesn't mean that they are a prophet or in an office of a prophet. I had the gift of prophecy way before God elevated me into the office of a prophet. For years, I worked in the hospital as a Registered Respiratory Therapist. Before God called me off that job, He had me in the hallway praying for people. That was totally out my comfort zone because I thought that was breaking all of my standards of professionalism. I was thinking, "God,

I am not a chaplain. I just can't ask my patients if they need prayer and preach to them."

But God had other plans. He broke my way of thinking and placed me in uncomfortable situations so I could do what He wanted me to do. It was an internal battle in my head and spirit because I was arguing with the Holy Spirit. Whenever, he told me to go pray for someone when I was working at the hospital initially I said "No, God I am not doing that!" I would get so convicted and feel such a burden that I had to give in. I was very stubborn, and God won. I learned over time just to obey him. One day, I lost my job in the hospital and I was very discouraged. I wanted to panic because I didn't know how I was going to survive without any income and I had two small kids to raise.

I didn't know what to do so I decided to work out to help release some tension. As I was on my elliptical machine, I heard God's voice. He said, "You are now in prophetic office." I was like what! For years, I was ministering prophetically, healing the sick, and casting out demons, but I was not in office. From that moment, God elevated me in the realm of the spirit. The mantle of a prophet fell upon me and I could feel it every time I got ready to minister. I started to have more supernatural encounters where physical winds would blow in my room out of nowhere, an increase amount of God's presence, signs, wonders, an increase word of knowledge and healing anointing.

My life changed. God had to show me that He was my sustainer and that he would take care of me. I no longer could depend on a secular job anymore, but be totally dependent on God for everything. God put me on a schedule. He gave me mandatory assignments of fasting, prayer, worship, projects such as books and programs, and even sent me to a local church to launch a prayer team, and to release a prophetic anointing there. Whenever you are in the office of a prophetic, there is more responsibility compared to someone that just has a gift. We will discuss more in detail the office of a prophet, how a prophet functions, and some things that they go through in the upcoming chapters. Remember, just because you are a prophesier does not make you a prophet. You probably just have the gift of prophecy.

The Greek word for the gift of prophecy is propheteia which is the ability to receive a divinely inspired message and deliver it to others in the church.[4] Help's Word Studies defines propheteia as prophecy, prophesying; the gift of communicating and enforcing revealed truth. Prophecies can take the form of exhortation, as we already discussed. It can also take the form of correction, like a rebuke. Prophecy can disclose secret sins because God knows the heart and the intents of our minds. In addition, prophecy can predict future events, comfort and inspire us. Subsequently, prophecy can include other revelations given to equip and edify the body of Christ. Prophecy has many dimensions and there are so many things to cover. You can get additional prophetic revelation from my upcoming series of books, "Enhancing the Prophetic in You."

1 Corinthians 14:1-5 says, "Follow after charity, and desire spiritual gifts, but rather that ye may prophesy. For he that speaketh in an unknown tongue speaketh not unto men, but

unto God: for no man understandeth him; howbeit in the spirit he speaketh mysteries. But he that prophesieth speaketh unto men to edification, and exhortation, and comfort. He that speaketh in an unknown tongue edifieth himself; but he that prophesieth edifieth the church. I would that ye all spake with tongues but rather that ye prophesied: for greater is he that prophesieth than he that speaketh with tongues, except he interpret, that the church may receive edifying."

We have already discussed some of the scriptures above, but I want to bring something to your attention. Prophecy and tongues are different. Speaking in tongues is not prophesying to an individual; you are speaking to God in a language only He understands. It is hard to understand when someone is prophesying to you and every other word that comes out their mouth is an unknown tongue. When students take my class, I immediately stop them. I break their habit of speaking in tongues like that when they are prophesying. Don't get me wrong, I am all for tongues. I believe that we should have prayed in tongues before class, in the morning, late at night, or throughout the day without ceasing.

Whenever you are prophesying, that is not the time to speak in tongues. That's an indication of a weak prophetic flow and that you have to build up your spirit man in order to prophesy. When you are prophesying, you want the recipient to understand what the Spirit of the Lord is speaking. You don't want them to be confused, because God is not the author of confusion but He a God of order. I train my students to be ready to prophesy in season and out of season. In other words, always be ready to prophesy because you never know when you'll have to. This is why it's so vital to have a prayer life and that includes praying in tongues consistently to build up yourself in the spirit (Jude 20) before class or your personal prayer time. If you are speaking in tongues between every other word then something is wrong with your prophetic flow. It needs to be cultivated.

Some churches will make the person who speaks in tongues interpret it so that the rest of church can understand what is being said in the spirit. I hope that brought some clarity. Now let's move forward. Did you know that prophecy can be used as a sign to an unbeliever? God wants to use prophecy to get some souls saved. If a sinner comes into your midst, God can show him or her that He is real by revealing all the secrets of their hearts and revealing awesome plans for their future. God doesn't want anyone to perish and go to hell. He would rather send a prophet in their path to warn them so they can repent and receive salvation. 1 Corinthians 14:24-25 says, "But if all prophesy, and there come in one that believeth not, or one unlearned, he is convinced of all, he is judged of all: And thus are the secrets of his heart made manifest; and so falling down on his face he will worship God, and report that God is in you of a truth."

Romans 12:6 says, "Having then gifts differing according to the grace that is given to us, whether prophecy, let us prophesy according to the proportion of faith;" Each one of us has a different grace for each of the gifts of the spirit. I always counsel my students to not flow like me or any other prophet. I tell them just to be themselves, because it's their uniqueness that sets them apart. It's their uniqueness that causes the maximum capability to reach the souls that they are able to reach. Whenever you copy off someone else, you are selling yourself short. God raises up originals, not copy-cats. Now, it takes faith to prophesy. The more faith you have, the greater that you are able to prophesy on a higher dimension in the realm of the spirit.

When I started off prophesying, I had a small amount of faith. I had to write everything I heard down on a sheet of paper then release it. I was afraid to miss because I didn't want people to call me a false prophet. It amazed me that all the words that I gave were accurate and it built up my confidence to prophesy. One day, I took a prophetic boot camp by Doctor Jimmie Reed and it changed my life. She really stretched me and her training launched me in the prophetic. This is why I stretch my students. I tell them that I did prophetic training and it helped me and I expect them to do it as well. After the prophetic boot camp, I had enough faith just to speak out what God placed in my mouth. I finally was flowing with the Holy Spirit on a new level. I believe those trials and prophetic training built up my faith in God just to allow Him to speak through me when I prophesy. There are times where I don't see or hear anything, I just open my mouth and God will fill it. Now that's faith to prophesy!

1 Peter 4:10-11 says, "As every man hath received the gift, even so minister the same one to another, as good stewards of the manifold grace of God. If any man speak, let him speak as the oracles of God; if any man minister, let him do it as of the ability which God giveth: that God in all things may be glorified through Jesus Christ, to whom be praise and dominion for ever and ever. Amen." We have to be good stewards of the gifts that

God gives us. We have to keep our gifts active and stirred. We want to be sharp in the spirit because it glorifies God. We need to prophesy in the spirit of excellence. We need to soar in the prophetic. Everything that we do for God we need to be good at it. The gift that God has given you is not for you but for others. We are called to serve one another with these gifts. Serving is true ministry.

Many people have asked me what does the word oracles mean? Notice how the word oracles looks similar to the word oral. Oral means the mouth cavity. Merriam Webster defines oracles as a person (as a priestess of ancient Greece) through whom a deity is believed to speak. We have to be confident and speak as God's oracles whenever He unctions us to speak. Now, we have covered the gift of prophecy, let's show an example of the gift of prophecy in action. Acts 21:9 says, "And the same man had four daughters, virgins, which did prophesy." This verse describes Phillip's four daughters. Phillip was an evangelist and his daughters weren't prophets but they had the gift. They just prophesied.

Prophetic Exercise: Pray and ask the Holy Spirit to show you something that will happen tomorrow in your day. Write it down. Journal about it. This will increase your faith and confidence in the prophetic.

Quick Review:

1) What is the gift of prophecy?

2)   What is the difference between the spirit of prophecy compared to the gift of prophecy?

3)   What is the difference between speaking in tongues and prophesying?

4)   Critical Thinking Question: What ways can you increase your faith to prophesy?

CHAPTER TEN

Office Of The Prophet

Now that we've discussed the spirit of prophecy and the gift of prophecy, let's discuss the office of the prophet. Many people feel that since they can prophesy, then they are in the office of a prophet. That is not true. You will know if you are in office because you will have some supernatural encounter with Jesus. In addition, men around you will see it or recognize that anointing on your life. So, in other words, God will confirm it and men will affirm it. Numbers 12:6 says, "And he said, Hear now my words: If there be a prophet among you, I the Lord will make myself known unto him in a vision, and will speak unto him in a dream." Many people allow men to push them into an office that they aren't anointed for. Then they wonder why they are facing so much spiritual warfare.

I always warn my students that if you put the title of Prophet or Prophetess in front of your name then you need to make sure that you have that anointing. The prophetic anointing attracts attacks. You will have to war against prophetic-level demons. Witches and warlocks will come seek after you. We will discuss more about prophets and warfare at the closing of this book. After God told me that I was a prophet, I began to have consecutive visions and trances. One day as I was praying, I kept seeing a man every time I closed my eyes. No matter what I did, I could not get this man out of my mind's eyes. I rebuked it and prayed against it, but it didn't work.

As I closed my eyes, I saw a man with a pure white face and white curly hair. Every part of his eyes were blood red. Out of his mouth was a long sword going in and out of it. I was frightened that the sword would poke me because of its length. He had a white garment on. At first I thought I was imagining things and I was unaware that I was seeing in the spirit realm and having a visitation from the Lord. I cried out, "Lord, what am I seeing?" The Holy Spirit replied and said, "You are seeing me in my Glory." I was puzzled. I was led to pick up my bible and immediately I went to Revelation chapter one.

What I saw amazed me. At this moment, I never read the book of Revelation so I didn't know what to expect. I avoided reading it because I was fearful of the end-times events that I heard people speak of. I began to read chapter one and I didn't get very far. My mouth dropped open because what I just read is what I had been seeing. Revelation 1:13-16 describes the son of man who is Jesus Christ. Maybe a few days later, I was worshipping laying prostrate on the floor in my living room in my former apartment.

As I lifted up my head, I saw Jesus Christ on a horse. He had a red cape on and a host of men that I perceived as angels on horses behind him. He spoke these chilling words to me. He said, "Tell my people I am coming back soon." I had many emotions flowing through me because these encounters weren't something I asked for. Once again, the Holy Spirit led me to book of Revelations. As I was reading chapter 19, I came across the vision that I had just seen (Revelation 19:11-16). Another encounter I had happened in the same time frame.

I was watching, "Sid Roth: It's Supernatural" one evening and the presence of God from that show came into my room. It was so overwhelming that I began to cry. I looked up by my front door and saw Jesus on the cross. He was bloody, bruised, and beaten beyond recognition yet I knew it was him. I got up from my chair, but the power of God was too strong. I dropped down on my knees and began to weep uncontrollably. I was watching the whole crucifixion occur right before my eyes. I even saw where the women went to the tomb to find Jesus but his body wasn't there. I saw where the angel asked, "Why do you seek the living among the dead?" Immediately, the scenery changed. I was standing on clouds. I could see Jesus walking towards me.

He wasn't bloody anymore. He was all clean and he had a long white garment on. He walked over to me and he placed a crown upon my head and a cloak or robe around me. As I looked down at my hands, I realized that they weren't my hands. They were the hands of Jesus. Both of my palms had a gigantic hole in them. Then the trance ended. My room felt like heaven. My body felt so pure and clean inside. After I gained my composure, the Holy Spirit lead me to Galatians 2:20. Galatians 2:20 says, "I am crucified with Christ: nevertheless I live; yet not I, but Christ liveth in me: and the life which I now live in the flesh I live by the faith of the Son of God, who loved me, and gave himself for me." At that moment, everything began to make sense. I saw the crucifixion because I was dying to myself and yielding fully to the Holy Spirit.

I can write a whole book on my encounters with God, but right now I want to focus on what a prophet is. After, I discovered that I was a prophet, God was calling me by giving me dreams and visions. It wasn't an easy transition, I encountered much warfare but God was right with me. You may be asking, "How are prophets are called?" Great question. It will be answered later in this book. To reiterate what was stated earlier, God will make himself know to someone who is a prophet either in a dream or vision. You will know without a shadow of a doubt that you are a prophet.

Prophets have two or three of the revelatory gifts of the spirit which we will discuss in the next chapter. Most prophets have a strong anointing for two of these three gifts: word of wisdom, word of knowledge, or discerning of spirits. The word of knowledge is my strongest gift, and it couples very well with the healing anointing on my life. Remember, if you have the gift of prophecy then you will just prophesy but rarely or never operate in the other gifts of the Holy Spirit. A person who is in prophetic office will have the strongest utterances because they speak by the spirit of prophecy, the gift of prophecy, and also out of the strength of their office. Someone with the gift of prophecy will speak prophecies of edification, exhortation, and comfort. People in the prophetic office have the grace to speak messages that go beyond words of edification, exhortation, and comfort.

> Ephesians 4:8-12 says, "Wherefore he saith, When he ascended up on high, he led captivity captive, and gave gifts unto men. (Now that he ascended, what is it but that he also descended first into the lower parts of the earth? He that descended is the same also that ascended up far above all heavens, that he might fill all things.) And he gave some, apostles; and some, prophets; and some, evangelists; and some, pastors and teachers; For the perfecting of the saints, for the work of the ministry, for the edifying of the body of Christ:"

Not everyone is in one of the fivefold offices listed in the scriptures above. If you are in office, you are a gift to the body of Christ and to the church. Your job is to equip the saints to do the work of ministry effectively not to build your empire. Whenever you are in one of these offices you are basically on the clock. Sometimes it's like going to a 9-5 job and you have tasks or assignments to conquer from the Holy Spirit. God is now your boss and you aren't dependent on a secular job but the Father himself. Not everyone is called off their secular jobs because God does call some of the fivefold to the marketplace.

Prophets prophesy with more authority than other believers who have not been called to the office of the prophet. They will read your mail and tell all your business. Their prophecies can carry revelation or new things from the Lord. Many people seek prophets for direction in life when they aren't able to hear from God from themselves. Prophets sometimes have to give words of correction or rebuke. I always tell people to beware of those so-called prophets who only speak things that tickle listening ears but never give a word of rebuke or preach on sin. A true prophet of God will preach against sin. God uses prophets to prophesy messages of confirmation of things that he has already spoken to a believer. God uses prophets to provide impartation of spiritual gifts to believers so they can do ministry more effectively. God also use prophets to activate certain gifts or anointing. In closing, prophets minister to a wider scope of needs than believers who speak by the spirit of prophecy or the simple gift of prophecy.

Prophetic Exercise: Pray and ask the Holy Spirit to reveal to you something in your heart and life that you need to work on or be delivered from. This will keep you a place of humility and heighten your awareness of accountability to the Holy Spirit.

Quick Review:

1) Define the office of a prophet.

2) How would someone know that they are called to the office of a prophet?

3) What ways does God use prophets?

4) Critical Thinking Question: Why is the ministry of the prophet important to the body of Christ?

CHAPTER ELEVEN

Gifts Of The Spirit

Gifts of the spirit are manifestations of the Holy Spirit. The Holy Spirit decides who gets what gifts or what measure of each gift they get. Jesus Christ decides who gets what office compared to the fivefold ministry (Ephesians 4:8-12). You don't have to have a title in front of your name such as Bishop or Apostle to have one of the gifts of the spirit. You can be a farmer, business man, or house wife. In other words, you can just be an average joe or the underdog and have the gifts of the spirit flowing powerfully through you. All believers should want and desire these gifts to do great exploits for the Lord. These gifts are supernatural and make the ministry God has given you more effective. You may say, "Well I am not in ministry?" Yes, you are. You are called to spread the gospel of Jesus Christ (Matthew 16:15-16). The word ministry means to serve. Diakonos is the Greek word for ministry[4]. You can serve other people in some capacity right where you are.

So many lives are depending on you to operate and embrace these gifts. Many people thank me for using the gifts that God has giving me to serve them. Remember these spiritual gifts are not for you but for others. 1 Peter 4:10 says, "As every man hath received the gift, even so minister the same one to another, as good stewards of the manifold grace of God." God has given us these gifts to serve others, so we need to be good stewards over what he has giving us. We have to exercise these gifts by keep them active and sharp. We have to close the door of sin in our lives and guard the anointing that God has placed upon us.

1 Corinthians 12:31 says, "But covet earnestly the best gifts: and yet shew I unto you a more excellent way." We need to desire the gifts of the spirit. Now the more excellent way that Apostle Paul was talking about was love. The next chapter is 1 Corinthians 13 which is talking about that if I operate in all these gifts but have not loved then I am nothing. I always tell my students that love makes the gifts work. What are your motives for wanting these spiritual gifts? Our aim for using these gifts as stated earlier is to Glory God and win souls for his kingdom. 1 Corinthians 1:7 says, "So that ye come behind in no gift; waiting for the coming of our Lord Jesus Christ:" It is not the will of God for us or the church to be lacking in any of these gifts. We have work to do and souls to save.

1 Corinthians 12:1-11 says, "Now concerning spiritual gifts, brethren, I would not have you ignorant. Ye know that ye were

Gentiles, carried away unto these dumb idols, even as ye were led. Wherefore I give you to understand, that no man speaking by the Spirit of God calleth Jesus accursed: and that no man can say that Jesus is the Lord, but by the Holy Ghost. Now there are diversities of gifts, but the same Spirit. And there are differences of administrations (ministries), but the same Lord (to serve the same Lord). And there are diversities of operations (actions, activities), but it is the same God which worketh all in all. But the manifestation of the Spirit is given to every man to profit withal (common good for everyone). For to one is given by the Spirit the word of wisdom; to another the word of knowledge by the same Spirit; To another faith by the same Spirit; to another the gifts of healing by the same Spirit; To another the working of miracles; to another prophecy; to another discerning of spirits; to another divers kinds of tongues; to another the interpretation of tongues: But all these worketh that one and the selfsame Spirit, dividing to every man severally as he will."

Apostle Paul, the author of the book of Corinthians, didn't want us to be ignorant of spiritual gifts. The devil destroys people by their ignorant or lack of knowledge (Hosea 4:6). Whenever a person discovers who they are in Christ and the amount of power and authority they possess, they become a threat to the devil. They don't have time to be led away by false religion like the early gentiles. They don't have time to blaspheme the Holy Spirit, but rather they are led by His spirit and they are about his agenda. There are different kinds of gifts but they all come from God. So many people are afraid of things they don't understand. These are the people that limit God and place Him in a box. The devil is a counterfeit and copycat of the original source, which is the power of God. When we look at the story of the staff of Aaron, the magicians were able to turn their staffs into serpents just like Aaron (Exodus 7:7-12). I recommend being open and relying on the Holy Spirit to bear witness of what is and isn't of him.

There are so many ministries that are so unique and different. They are called to reach so many people of different backgrounds and various needs. Yet they all are under our Lord and Savior Jesus Christ. Each ministry is important and part of the body of Christ. For instance, some ministries focus on the youth, some on marriages, some on prophecy, some on healing, etc., yet they all serve God. Just because these ministries are different and do different things doesn't mean that they aren't led by the Holy Spirit. They just have a different assignment from you. The gifts of the spirit are to benefit everyone.

Before we discuss each of the gifts of the spirit, lets divide them into three groups for greater clarity and understanding. The nine gifts can be divided into three groups of three: revelatory gifts, power gifts, and vocal gifts. The revelation gifts are word of wisdom, word of knowledge, and discerning of spirits. The power gifts are the gift of faith, gifts of healings, and workings of miracles. The vocal gifts are tongues, and the interpretation of tongues, and the gift of prophecy. Remember, that prophets have two of the three revelatory gifts operating really strong through them.

The first gift that we will discuss is the word of wisdom. Many people confuse this gift with the word of knowledge. Wisdom is directive or has some instructions attached to it. Knowledge is informative or enlightening information. Wisdom and knowledge are interdependent. Wisdom needs knowledge upon which to act. Wisdom is profitable to direct. Ecclesiastes 10:10 says, "If the iron be blunt, and he do not whet the edge, then must he put to more strength: but wisdom is profitable to direct." Let's look at a few examples of the word of wisdom. Evangelist Philip was directed to Gaza to speak to the Ethiopian Eunuch who didn't understand the biblical passage he was reading. Since Philip obeyed the Holy Spirit, the eunuch was saved and baptized (Acts. 8:26–29). In 1 Kings 3:16-28 we can see where King Solomon operated in the word of wisdom to settle the dispute between the two women over whose son it was.

The next gift that we will discuss is the word of knowledge. The word of knowledge often gets confused with prophecy. The two are different. The word of knowledge is a supernatural fact about someone that is past or current. It can manifest in many ways. It can be an impression on your body which indicates pain or sickness that the person you are ministering to is undergoing. You can also feel what they feel. It can be names, birthdates, addresses, phone number, social security numbers, and the list goes on. To sum of the word of knowledge, it is a supernatural knowing of something. Jesus operated in the word of knowledge in John 4:16–19 when he revealed that the Samaritan woman had five husbands. She ended up getting convicted and became an evangelist. She told everyone about Jesus. Apostle Peter operated in the word of knowledge when he revealed what Ananias and Sapphira had done and they dropped dead (Acts 5:1–11). In Acts 9:11–12, Ananias received knowledge of Saul.

The last revelatory gift that we will discuss is the discerning of spirits. This gift is recognizing and distinguishing the difference between different spirits. This gift needs to be cultivated by exercising the spirit senses. Hebrews 5:14 says, "But strong meat belongeth to them that are of full age, even those who by reason of use have their senses exercised to discern both good and evil." People with this gift are able to discern what kind of spirits a person has. They are able to discern different demonic spirits, angels, or what is part of the Holy Spirit. In John 1:32–33, John the Baptist discerns the Holy Spirit upon Jesus as a dove. In Acts 2:3, The believers in the upper room discern the Holy Spirit as tongues of fire. In Matthew 9:32–34, Jesus was able to discern a dumb spirit.

Let's move on to the power gifts now. Many people get the gifts of working of miracles and healings confused. Healings are usually gradual. For instance, if someone prays for someone to be healed of cancer and it goes away within months is considered healing. However, if someone prays for a lump to disappear and it shrinks right before your eyes then that is considered a miracle. The Greek word for miracle is dunamis[4]. It means might, power, or marvelous works. The gift of working of miracles is the ability to demonstrate the supernatural power of the Holy Spirit. Let's look at some examples of the gift of miracles. In John 2:6–11, Jesus turns water into wine. In John 6:8–14, Jesus multiplies the loaves and fishes. In John 9:1–7, Jesus anoints a blind man's eyes with clay and restores his sight.

The next power gift that we will discuss is the gift of healings. Notice that healings is plural. There are various kinds of healings. Some ministries may have a healing anointing for cancer where you witness lots of people getting healed from cancer in that ministry. Some ministries may have a healing anointing for arthritis and you are able to witness many people getting healed from that. Some ministries may have an anointing to heal asthma and many healings of asthma or other respiratory ailments get healed. The list goes on and on. In Luke 4:40, Jesus lays His hands on every one and heals them. In Matthew, 8:1–3, Jesus touches and heals a leper. In Mark 7:32–35, Jesus heals a man of deafness and a speech impediment.

The last power gift that we will discuss is the gift of faith. This is supernatural faith that is imparted by the Holy Spirit. When this faith comes upon a believer they can believe God for the impossible and witness God do the impossible. In other words, it's having more than the usual faith and confidence in God's power so He can do great works through an individual. In Mark 4:39–41, Jesus calms the storm. This had to take great faith in order to produce supernatural results and the winds and the sea had no other choice but to comply. In Luke 7:12–15, Jesus raises the widow's son. It takes faith in order to speak life into someone who was just deceased and to see them come alive again. The same applies to the next example. In Luke 8:54–55, Jesus raises the daughter of Jairus. I always tell my students that faith is the currency for everything in the kingdom of God.

Now we will discuss the vocal gifts. We have already discussed the gift of prophecy previously so we will discuss the gift of tongues and tongue interpretation. The gift of tongues or diverse tongues (1 Corinthians 12:28) is the supernatural ability to speak a foreign language that the tongues-speaker had never learned. In Acts 2:4–12, as the Jews in Jerusalem heard the gospel preached in a wide variety of languages. Think of the word "tongues" as languages. 1 Corinthians 14:6 says, "Now, brethren, if I come unto you speaking with tongues, what shall I profit you, except I shall speak to you either by revelation, or by knowledge, or by prophesying, or by doctrine?" To paraphrase what Apostle Paul was saying in 1 Corinthians 14:6, "How can I help you by speaking tongues unless I bring some type of revelation or interpret it?" Tongues are valuable for the recipient hearing God's message in their own language but it needs to be interpreted for everyone else. Now, tongues build yourself up in your faith (Jude 20) and makes intercession for oneself (Romans 8:26).

Let's now discuss the next vocal gift which is the interpretation of tongues. The gift of interpreting tongues is the ability to translate a foreign language into the language of the hearers. A person with the gift of interpreting tongues, then, could understand what a tongues-speaker was saying even though he did not know the language being spoken. 1 Corinthians 14:27 says, "If any man speak in an unknown tongue, let it be by two, or at the most by three, and that by course; and let one interpret." 1 Corinthians 14:13 says, "Wherefore let him that speaketh in an unknown tongue pray that he may interpret." There were times, that I interpret my own tongues as I was worshipping. Step out in faith and ask God to give you the interpretation of your tongues or tongues of others and you will be surprised.

This gift is important and helps to keep order and ensure that everyone is in one accord.

Let's look at more spiritual gifts. 1 Corinthians 7:7 says, "For I would that all men were even as I myself. But every man hath his proper gift of God (but each person has his own gift from God), one after this manner, and another after that." This is apostle Paul speaking. This scripture is also given as reference for the gift of celibacy. Celibacy is abstaining from marriage or sex.[7] 1 Corinthians 7:32-34 says, "But I would have you without carefulness. He that is unmarried careth for the things that belong to the Lord, how he may please the Lord: But he that is married careth for the things that are of the world, how he may please his wife. There is difference also between a wife and a virgin. The unmarried woman careth for the things of the Lord, that she may be holy both in body and in spirit: but she that is married careth for the things of the world, how she may please her husband." Apostle Paul said that when we are single we can get more done for the Lord compare to someone that's married because they have to divide their time between God and their spouse.

Romans 12:6-8 says, "Having then gifts differing according to the grace that is given to us, whether prophecy, let us prophesy according to the proportion of faith; Or ministry, let us wait on our ministering (serve): or he that teacheth, on teaching; Or he that exhorteth (encourage), on exhortation: he that giveth, let him do it with simplicity; he that ruleth (lead), with diligence; he that sheweth mercy, with cheerfulness." Each one of us have been given a different measure of grace to operate in these spiritual gifts. We just need to be ourselves and don't try to flow like someone else. It takes faith to prophesy. There are different gifts mentioned in Romans 12. There is the gift of teaching. This gift is important because teachers bring a greater understanding and depth to the word for others who may lack comprehension. There is the gift of encouragement. This gift is important because so many people are weary and need to hear a word of cheer. There is the gift of giving, which is important to finance the work of the Lord. There is a gift of leading or ruling which the person is able to lead effectively in wisdom. There is the gift of mercy which is important for the believers who have fallen to be restored back into the body of Christ.

1 Corinthians 12:28 says, "And God hath set some in the church, first apostles, secondarily prophets, thirdly teachers, after that miracles, then gifts of healings, helps, governments, diversities of tongues." There is also the gifts of helps which is always having the desire and ability to help others, to do whatever it takes to get a task accomplished. This gift is important because one person can't complete the task by themselves. There is also the gifts of government or administration which is being able to keep things organized and in accordance with God's principles. Every ministry needs this gift in order to keep organized and to keep things orderly. There is also the gift of righteousness (Romans 5:17) and eternal life (Romans 6:23).

Prophetic Exercise: Pray and ask the Holy Spirit to reveal to you the spirit gifts that you have operating in your life.

Quick Review:

1) Define spiritual gifts.

2) Name the different gifts of the spirit and other spiritual gifts.

3) Why are spiritual gifts important?

4) Critical Thinking Question: What ways can you exercise the spiritual gifts in your life?

CHAPTER TWELVE

Functions Of A Prophet

Many people believe that prophets go around prophesying all day. However, that's not true. Prophets do much more than prophesy. Let's go through some of the functions prophets have. The ministry of a prophet is not a glamorous one. They go through much warfare, rejection, and loneliness. They have to get away from the crowd to hear from God. The ministry of the prophet is vital to the body of Christ because most of its spend on their knees in prayer. Once, I asked God what my assignment was and He said, "To pray and intercede." Prophets must pray. The first function of a prophet is prayer.

Prophets need to have a consistent prayer life. Daniel was a prophet and he prayed three times a day. Daniel 6:10 says, "Now when Daniel knew that the writing was signed, he went into his house; and his windows being open in his chamber toward Jerusalem, he kneeled upon his knees three times a day, and prayed, and gave thanks before his God, as he did aforetime." Habakkuk was a prophet who prayed and rejoiced in Habakkuk chapter 3. Joel the prophet interceded when there was a locust invasion (Joel 1:19-20).

Prophets have to be patient to receive the word of the Lord. They must spend time in prayer and on their faces in order to hear from God. Most of the time when I receive a revelatory word from God, I have been in His presence and waited to hear what He had to say. This is the time where I am not speaking but asking God, "Lord, what's on your heart and what do I need to pray for?" The bible warns us of false prophets who are speaking things that God has not spoken. They have not been in God's counsel. Jeremiah 23:18 says, "For who hath stood in the counsel of the LORD, and hath perceived and heard his word? who hath marked his word, and heard it?" God did not send these false prophets who prophesied lies in His name. Jeremiah 23:21-22 says, "I have not sent these prophets, yet they ran: I have not spoken to them, yet they prophesied. But if they had stood in my counsel, and had caused my people to hear my words, then they should have turned them from their evil way, and from the evil of their doings." As a prophet, it is vital to wait for God's counsel before you speak. Let's look at some examples of prophets who waited on God's counsel. 2 Kings 20:16, "And Isaiah said unto Hezekiah, Hear the word of the LORD." The prophet Isaiah prophesied to Hezekiah the King after the messengers from Babylon came to visit. Jeremiah 15:16 says, "Your words were found and I ate them, And Your words became for me a joy and the delight of my heart; For I have been called by Your name, O LORD God of hosts." Jeremiah was always in a posture to hear what the spirit of the Lord was saying. 2 Samuel 23:2 says, "The Spirit of the LORD spoke by me, And His word was on my tongue." The prophet Samuel's ways pleased the Lord, he developed a closer relationship with him and the word of the Lord was in his mouth.

Prophets have to suffer at times. They suffer from the persecution, trials, loneliness, isolations, and the rejection they experience. I had to suffer to get the anointing that is upon my life. Once, I lost everything and everyone in my life. Now, the Lord is restoring things back to me. It wasn't until I suffered that I realized that Jesus understands and I was suffering for the gospel's sake. Hebrews 4:15 says, "For we have not an high priest which cannot be touched with the feeling of our infirmities; but was in all points tempted like as we are, yet without sin." It seems the more you do right, the more the attacks come. 2 Timothy 3:12 says, "Yea, and all that will live godly in Christ Jesus shall suffer persecution." 1 Peter 4:1 says, "Forasmuch then as Christ hath suffered for us in the flesh, arm yourselves likewise with the same mind: for he that hath suffered in the flesh hath ceased from sin;" Jesus was a prophet and he suffered. Ezekiel had to suffer as well, the Lord took away his wife who brought him happiness, joy, and pleasure as a prophetic sign of what the Lord will do to the people (Ezekiel 24:15-27). Jeremiah the prophet suffered because people lied on him and refused to listen to the prophetic word (Jeremiah 18:18). He was mocked and ridiculed (Jeremiah 20:7). He was put in stocks (Jeremiah 20:2), chained

(Jeremiah 40:1), and placed in a pit and left to die, though rescued (Jeremiah 38:6-13).

Prophets are called to worship. How can you be a prophet not worship? When you worship, you are loving on God, serving, and ministering to him. Let's look at Acts 13:2 in three different translations.

Acts 13:2 (EXB) says, "They were all ·worshiping [or serving] the Lord and fasting [giving up eating for spiritual purposes]. During this time the Holy Spirit said to them, "Set apart for me Barnabas and Saul to do the special [the] work for which I have chosen [called] them."

Acts 13:2 (NASB) says, "While they were ministering to the Lord and fasting, the Holy Spirit said, "Set apart for Me Barnabas and Saul for the work to which I have called them."

Acts 13:2 NIV says, "While they were worshiping the Lord and fasting, the Holy Spirit said, "Set apart for me Barnabas and Saul for the work to which I have called them."

2 Chronicles 29:30 says, "Moreover Hezekiah the king and the princes commanded the Levites to sing praise unto the LORD with the words of David, and of Asaph the seer. And they sang praises with gladness, and they bowed their heads and worshipped." King David who himself was a prophet was surrounded by other prophets. Asaph was a worshiper and a prophet and he ministered before the Lord continually. 1 Chronicles 16:37 says, "So he left there before the ark of the covenant of the Lord Asaph and his brethren, to minister before the ark continually,

as every day's work required:" Heman and Jeduthun were also other prophets who worshipped (1 Chronicles 25).

Prophets encourage others. Judas and Silas were prophets that encouraged the believers at Antioch (Acts 15:32). No matter how bad things get, the prophet has a special ability to be the eyes and the mouth of God. They can see the positivity of the things God is doing in the midst of calamity. Their prophecies aren't always judgment but sometimes balanced with the promises of the Lord. In the book of Habakkuk, the first two chapter were judgment yet in the last and third chapter the prophecies were ones of hope. I always tell my students that their prophecies need to be balance. The reason for judgment words sometimes is to give a way out so the recipient can repent. Once they repent, there needs to be an avenue of hope. Remember, God is merciful and He doesn't want anyone to perish.

Prophets have the ability to foretell the future. Most of the prophets of old predicted the coming of the Messiah years or centuries before He came in the flesh. Let's look at the book of Zechariah. I always tell people that this is my favorite prophet because of his special grace to interact with angels and the night time visions that he received. Zechariah talks about Christ's entrance into Jerusalem on a colt. Zechariah 9:9 says, "Rejoice greatly, O daughter of Zion; shout, O daughter of Jerusalem: behold, thy King cometh unto thee: he is just, and having salvation; lowly, and riding upon an ass, and upon a colt the foal of an ass." Zechariah even foretold Jesus being betrayed for 30 pieces of silver. Zechariah 11:12 says, "And I said unto them, If ye think good, give me my price; and if not, forbear. So they weighed for my price thirty pieces of silver." He even saw the Messiah being pierced. Zechariah 12:10 says, "And I will pour upon the house of David, and upon the inhabitants of Jerusalem, the spirit of grace and of supplications: and they shall look upon me whom they have pierced, and they shall mourn for him, as one mourneth for his only son, and shall be in bitterness for him, as one that is in bitterness for his firstborn." Lastly, he even had a vision about the Branch coming or the Messiah coming (Zechariah 3:1-10) and prophesied about the Branch (Messiah) building the temple of God (Zechariah 6:9-15).

Many people seek prophets for direction and guidance. When people come to my prophetic calls, the number one thing they say is that they need direction and guidance. Sometimes we get overwhelmed by the trials in life and lose sight of the promises of God and allow our minds to be clouded by doubt. It takes a prophet to speak what God is doing, what God is going to do, and what the people or church should do next? Gad was David's prophet and his words provided direction and guidance for the king. 1 Samuel 22:5 says, "And the prophet Gad said unto David, Abide not in the hold; depart, and get thee into the land of Judah. Then David departed, and came into the forest of Hareth." Young Saul before he was chosen to be King, sought the prophet to find out what happened to his father's lost donkeys (1 Samuel 9:18-19).

Prophets have a special anointing to interpret dreams and visions. The basic definition of a seer is someone who has frequent dreams and visions from the Lord. 1 Samuel 9:9 says, "Beforetime in Israel, when a man went to enquire of God, thus he spake, Come, and let us go to the seer: for he that is now called a Prophet was beforetime called a Seer." Whenever God shows you something, that is considered revelation. It is our job to ask for the interpretation. We can see this pattern consistently in the book of Zechariah. Whenever he had a night vision, he would always ask God for the interpretation and the angel of the Lord would be there to interpret it. Once we receive the interpretation, we need to apply it or put forth application. After that we are able to get manifestations. Daniel was a prophet who was able to interpret dreams. Nebuchadnezzar had a troubling dream and threaten to kill all the wise men in Babylon unless someone would tell him what he dreamed and the meaning of it. Daniel sought God and reveal the dream and interpret it (Daniel 2). Joseph was another prophet who was able to interpret the Pharaoh's dream (Genesis 41).

Prophets sometimes have to give words of rebuke or correction. The word admonition means a gentle or friendly reproof, counsel, or warning against fault or oversight[8]. A true prophet is grieved by sin and the things that burden the Lord. Jeremiah 1:10 says, "See, I have this day set thee over the nations and over the kingdoms, to root out, and to pull down, and to destroy, and to throw down, to build, and to plant." Prophets have to root out or pull out negativity, strongholds, falsehoods, or anything not of God. They also have to tear down the demonic opposition which includes religious spirits and things that try to prevent the move of God. Prophets have to destroy and overthrow some things that are not build upon the true foundation of the word of God before they can build or plant. This all involves giving words of rebuke or correction. Elijah the prophet had to confront and kill the false prophets of Baal (1 Kings 18).

Prophets are called to expose rotten leadership. They are God pleasers, not people pleasers. They aren't worried about being popular. Hosea had to prophesy against false prophets and bad leaders. Hosea 4:5 says, "Therefore shalt thou fall in the day, and the prophet also shall fall with thee in the night, and I will destroy thy mother." Micah had to prophesy against false prophets as well (Micah 3:6-7). Ezekiel 13:1 says, "And the word of the Lord came unto me, saying, Son of man, prophesy against the prophets of Israel that prophesy, and say thou unto them that prophesy out of their own hearts, Hear ye the word of the Lord; Thus saith the Lord God; Woe unto the foolish prophets, that follow their own spirit, and have seen nothing!" We can also see that the prophet Ezekiel had to prophesy against false leadership as well. Zephaniah and Hosea prophesied against idolatrous priests (Zephaniah 1:4 and Hosea 10:5). When you are called as a prophet, you need to pray to be bold in the Lord so you can do what you are called to do.

God is just and his judgment is fair. He sends prophets in hostile environments at time just to get word out. Psalm 33:5 says, "He loveth righteousness and judgment: the earth is full of the goodness of the LORD." However, sometimes people listen and sometimes they don't take heed. Prophets are called to announce judgment. Let's look at the two prophets who were called to go to Nineveh. Nahum had to pronounce judgment against Nineveh and the people didn't take heed. It is not our job as prophets to worry about who receives the word of the

Lord or not. Our job is to deliver the word and leave it between God and the recipient.

God speaks to his prophets in various ways. He doesn't do anything in the earth realm without showing his prophets. Amos 3:7 says, "Surely the Lord God will do nothing, but he revealeth his secret unto his servants the prophets." Prophets have to warn people of danger. We are called to intercede over the things God shows us. Genesis 18:17 says, "And the LORD said, Shall I hide from Abraham that thing which I do;" God didn't want to destroy Sodom until he told his friend Abraham. Acts 21:10-11 says, "And as we tarried there many days, there came down from Judaea a certain prophet, named Agabus. And when he was come unto us, he took Paul's girdle, and bound his own hands and feet, and said, Thus saith the Holy Ghost, So shall the Jews at Jerusalem bind the man that owneth this girdle, and shall deliver him into the hands of the Gentiles." The prophets Agabus warns Apostle Paul that if he goes to Jerusalem he would be bounded there. He used a prophetic demonstration to get this message across by bounding up his own hands and feet with Apostle Paul's belt.

Prophets need to be in tune with the spirit of the Lord to be able to understand and interpret the signs of the times. We don't need to be panic when the world is falling apart. We need to have confidence in our God and trust Him fully. 1 Chronicles 12:32 says, "And of the children of Issachar, which were men that had understanding of the times, to know what Israel ought to do; the heads of them were two hundred; and all their brethren were at their commandment." Just like the sons of Issachar, when you understand the times, you know what you ought to do. Esther 1:13 says, "Then the king said to the wise men, which knew the times, (for so was the king's manner toward all that knew law and judgment." Whenever you know the times, you will have divine access to people of influence and people will seek after you for the wisdom that you carry. Jesus rebuked the Jews because they couldn't understand the times (Luke 12:54-56). The prophet Elijah was able to discern a rain cloud way in the spirit before there were any rain clouds physically in the sky (1 Kings 18:41-43).

Have you ever pondered about who wrote the Pentateuch, the first five books of the bible? Moses is known to get credit with this authorship. How could he have known such great details such as the names, locations, and the significant events that transpired throughout history? He had to know his history and rely on the Holy Spirit for revelation. Prophets can't be ignorant about the things that are occurring around them and even the things that happened in past generations. We have to be studious of the word of God and need to know what to pray for and against. Ephesians 3:5 says, "Which in other ages was not made known unto the sons of men, as it is now revealed unto his holy apostles and prophets by the Spirit."

Prophets are sensitive to the presence of God. They are able to discern and test prophecy. Prophets are called to judge prophecy. 1 Corinthians 14:29 says, "Let the prophets speak two or three, and let the other judge." This is why it is vital for prophets to have a strong foundation of the word to be able to separate the wheat from the tares or the good from the junk. Prophets need to judge prophecy to help keep order in the church and to eliminate confusion and disorder. I always tell people to judge my prophecies because I believe in accountability. If someone doesn't want their prophetic words judged then watch out because that person is operating in error. God will never speak anything that goes against his word and his word will come to pass. However, there were times that his word didn't come to pass but it was only because he changed his mind because the people repented. One example of this is in the book of Jonah. God didn't destroy Nineveh because the people repented. Jonah wasn't a false prophet but an immature one because he was stubborn and angry when the people repented.

Prophets are called to be watchmen. Every biblical city had a stronghold or a fortified wall built around the city. The stronghold had watch towers where an appointed watchman sounded the alarm or blew the trumpet or ram's horn when he spotted danger. This is why God wakes us up in the middle of the night to pray and intercede for one another and to cancel the schemes of the devil. The prophet Ezekiel was a watchman and it was a big responsibility. He knew that if he wasn't on his post then that blood would be on his hands if he didn't warn the people (Ezekiel 33:1-11). Get back on the post, watchmen and stop falling asleep when it's time to pray!

Many prophets in the bible had to prophesy against nations. They had words for nations and they pronounced the judgment of God upon them for their sins. Look at the book of Obadiah. He had to prophesy against the Edomites because they were in treachery. Inside of helping their fallen brother

Israel, they kicked them and helped them get in captivity. God was enraged and used his prophet Obadiah to prophesy against them. Look at Micah chapter 1 versus 11 through 13. Micah had to give words to the inhabitants of Saphir, Zaanan, Maroth, and Lachish. Isaiah prophesied against nations (Isaiah 13-12), so did Jeremiah (Jeremiah 46-51), and Ezekiel (Ezekiel 25-32). Whenever you challenge a nation, you confront leaders, kings, presidents, governors, etc. and take part in political affairs.

Prophets initiates God's actions and plans. The word initiate means to cause or facilitate the beginning of or set going[9]. Let's look at 2 Kings 9. One of Elisha's students or proteges was instructed to anoint Jehu and prophesy that he would be King over Israel. When this occurred, a chain reaction set off. Jehu told the company of men what the prophet spoke and they agreed and made him King. Jehu began to fulfil the prophecy that Elijah spoke over Ahab. Jehu took down Ahab's son, Joram, King Ahaziah, Jezebel, and the seventy sons of Ahab. Isaiah prophesied what the Lord had spoken to initiate God's action (Isaiah 14:24-27).

Prophets are the spokesman of God. They explain what must be done. They can speak how God wants to bring change out of the tragedies and the devastations that are occurring worldwide. For instance, when attacks of terrorism and hate crimes increase, the prophets are the ones calling corporate fasting and prayer meetings to seek God to see what the spirit of the Lord is saying. These prophets have the peace of God because they have already seen the end results and the great things that God wants to do. They aren't caught up in sight, but they walk by faith.

Prophets need to be good theologians. Theology is the study of religious faith, practice, and experience; especially or the study of God and of God's relation to the world[10]. The prophet Daniel was a good theologian. He knew the word of God and he even prayed out the prophecies of Jeremiah. He was very aware of the prophecies of old. Daniel 9:2 says, "In the first year of his reign I Daniel understood by books the number of the years, whereof the word of the LORD came to Jeremiah the prophet, that he would accomplish seventy years in the desolations of Jerusalem." Prophets need to be full of the revelation of God's word. Daniel decided to war over these prophecies in prayer. Daniel 9:3 says, "And I set my face unto the Lord God, to seek by prayer and supplications, with fasting, and sackcloth, and ashes."

Some prophets operate in miracles, but some don't. John the Baptist didn't operate in miracles, but Jesus called him the greatest of all prophets (Matthew 11:11). Abraham didn't prophesy, but he was a mighty prophet. Some prophets have healing anointing to heal the sick. Jesus healed the sick (Matthew 8), Elisha raised the dead (2 Kings 4:32-35), Elisha's word healed Naaman of leprosy (2 Kings 5:7-10), Abraham prayed to God, and God healed Abimelech (Genesis 20:17), and God inflicted Miriam with leprosy and Moses interceded for her (Numbers 12). Some prophetic mantles come with healing.

Some prophets have to appoint and anoint leaders. Prophets have a special ability to impart. 1 Timothy 4:14 says, "Neglect not the gift that is in thee, which was given thee by prophecy, with the laying on of the hands of the presbytery." Samuel the prophet anointed Saul King (1 Samuel 10) and he anointed

David King (1 Samuel 16). 1 Kings 1:34 says, "And let Zadok the priest and Nathan the prophet anoint him their king over Israel: and blow ye with the trumpet, and say, God save king Solomon." Nathan the prophet anointed Solomon to be King. Elijah appointed Elisha as his protégé (1 Kings 19). Some prophets have access to the kings or leaders. They are called to advise kings and political leaders. Nathan the prophet advised king David (2 Samuel 7) and Gad advised King David as well (1 Samuel 22:5, 2 Samuel 24). The wicked King Ahab sought prophets to see if he should go into battle (1 Kings 20). Elisha was able to speak the plans of the enemy and warn the king of the enemy's plans (2 Kings 6:9-12).

Some prophets are good historians. They are called to be scribes and record the events of times. We can see this in several places in the bible. 2 Chronicles 26:22 says, "Now the rest of the acts of Uzziah, first and last, did Isaiah the prophet, the son of Amoz, write." Isaiah wrote down the events of the King Uzziah. 2 Chronicles 13:22 says, "And the rest of the acts of Abijah, and his ways, and his sayings, are written in the story of the prophet Iddo." The prophet Iddo wrote down what occurred in the days of King Abijah. 1 Chronicles 29:29-30 says, "Now the acts of David the king, first and last, behold, they are written in the book of Samuel the seer, and in the book of Nathan the prophet, and in the book of Gad the seer, With all his reign and his might, and the times that went over him, and over Israel, and over all the kingdoms of the countries." The prophet Samuel, Nathan, and Gad wrote down the things that King David did in his days.

Prophets have angels assigned to them and their ministries. Moses had an angel to help guide him in the wilderness and to protect him and his people (Exodus 23:20-26). Daniel 6:22 says, "My God hath sent his angel, and hath shut the lions' mouths, that they have not hurt me: forasmuch as before him innocence was found in me; and also before thee, O king, have I done no hurt." When Daniel was in trouble and facing death, God sent an angel. Jacob wrestled with an angel and got a blessing (Genesis 32:22-31). Zechariah had an angel who continually gave him revelation of his night time visions (Zechariah 4 and 5).

Prophetic Exercise: Pray and ask the Holy Spirit to show you someone that you will cross paths with that you can win them over to the body of Christ. Ask the Holy Spirit for a word of knowledge for them. This is an exercise to practice prophetic evangelism. God may show you someone in a pink shirt that you will meet at McDonalds. When you see the person, step out in faith and begin to minister to them.

Quick Review:

1) What are some functions of a prophet?

2) How important is it to be knowledgeable of the lifestyle and the functions of a prophet?

3) Why must prophets be patient to receive the word of the Lord?

4) Critical Thinking Question: How can you strengthen the functions that were discuss in this chapter in your own life?

CHAPTER THIRTEEN

Call of A Prophet

Prophets are called in many different ways. God chooses whom he wants and gives them different assignments. You don't have to have other prophets in your family to be called. You don't have to have the perfect background for God to call you. Though the biblical prophets have some similarities, there are vast differences. I was called as a prophet when I had a wilderness experience. This was a perfect time for God to call me and for me to accept the call because prior I had no interest in serving God and I wanted to follow my own agenda. It wasn't until I hit rock bottom that I sought God. I found comfort in studying the lives of biblical prophets because I could relate some of my encounters to some of the encounters they experienced.

Some people are called as a prophet in the womb. Jeremiah 1:4-5 says, "Then the word of the Lord came unto me, saying,

Before I formed thee in the belly I knew thee; and before thou camest forth out of the womb I sanctified thee, and I ordained thee a prophet unto the nations." This means that certain prophets were ordained to be prophets before they were born. God had a plan for their lives and He normally calls them at a young age just like the prophet Jeremiah. Jeremiah was hesitant at first because he felt that he was only a child but the Lord told him that he would be with him to deliver him.

Some people are called as prophets during childhood. Samuel began to hear the voice of God at very young age. His mother Hannah dedicated Him to God and he was raised in the temple by Eli the priest. One day, God began to call Samuel but he was unable to recognize God's voice but thought it was Eli calling him. Eli finally perceived what was going on and told him that it was God calling him. God told young prophet Samuel that was going to be judgment on Eli's house (1 Samuel 3).

Isaiah 6:1-8 (KJV) In the year that king Uzziah died I saw also the Lord sitting upon a throne, high and lifted up, and his train filled the temple. Above it stood the seraphims: each one had six wings; with twain he covered his face, and with twain he covered his feet, and with twain he did fly. And one cried unto another, and said, Holy, holy, holy, is the Lord of hosts: the whole earth is full of his glory. And the posts of the door moved at the voice of him that cried, and the house was filled with smoke. Then said I, Woe is me! for I am undone; because I am a man of unclean lips, and I dwell in the midst of a people of unclean lips: for mine eyes have seen the King, the Lord of hosts. Then flew one of the seraphims unto me, having a live coal in his hand, which he had taken with the tongs from off the altar: And he laid it upon my mouth, and said, Lo, this hath touched thy lips; and thine iniquity is taken away, and thy sin purged. Also I heard the voice of the Lord, saying, Whom shall I send, and who will go for us? Then said I, Here am I; send me.

Let's look at the book of Isaiah. Isaiah wasn't called until the sixth chapter. He probably had the gift of prophecy but in the sixth chapter that is when he had a throne room encounter. This is a wonderful experience to witness God sitting upon a throne. Once I seen God sitting on a throne but I couldn't see his face because it was full of light just like the sun. I saw a man dressed in white who was enormous. This encounter is on my website. When I read about Isaiah's encounter, I realized that I wasn't crazy but it was biblical. I was glad to find an experience to the one I had. In Isaiah's vision, the Lord had a long robe that filled the glorious temple. There were many heavenly creatures that the prophet witness who are known as fiery ones or seraphim. They have six wings and they cry out, "Holy" day and night around the throne of God. Seraphim symbolize purity because the first thing they did was clean out Isaiah's mouth with a tong carrying hot coal. God deals with the mouth of the prophet first because we are his oracles. There is nothing worse than a cursing prophet. Cursing shows a sign of immaturity. When Isaiah was in God's glory, he immediately felt unclean and cried out that he was a man of unclean lips. After this encounter, God sent the prophet out.

Jeremiah 1:4-10 (KJV) Then the word of the Lord came unto

me, saying, Before I formed thee in the belly I knew thee; and before thou camest forth out of the womb I sanctified thee, and I ordained thee a prophet unto the nations. Then said I, Ah, Lord God! behold, I cannot speak: for I am a child. But the Lord said unto me, Say not, I am a child: for thou shalt go to all that I shall send thee, and whatsoever I command thee thou shalt speak. Be not afraid of their faces: for I am with thee to deliver thee, saith the Lord. Then the Lord put forth his hand, and touched my mouth. And the Lord said unto me, Behold, I have put my words in thy mouth. See, I have this day set thee over the nations and over the kingdoms, to root out, and to pull down, and to destroy, and to throw down, to build, and to plant.

Jeremiah got called as a youth. Some prophets get called later on in life as adults. Jeremiah felt inadequate because of his age but the Lord reassured him and told him that he was chosen before birth. The Lord told the prophet that he will be with him and not to be afraid of the enemy because God will deliver him. Notice, how God touched Jeremiah's mouth and filled it with his words. He called Jeremiah to be rule over nations and kingdoms to root up and destroy things not of God before he could build it on the foundation of God and plant the word.

Amos 7:12-16 (KJV) Also Amaziah said unto Amos, O thou seer, go, flee thee away into the land of Judah, and there eat bread, and prophesy there: But prophesy not again any more at Bethel: for it is the king's chapel, and it is the king's court. Then answered Amos, and said to Amaziah, I was no prophet, neither was I a prophet's son; but I was an herdman, and a gatherer of sycomore fruit: And the Lord took me as I followed the flock, and the Lord said unto me, Go, prophesy unto my people Israel. Now therefore hear thou the word of the Lord: Thou sayest, Prophesy not against Israel, and drop not thy word against the house of Isaac.

Amos is a prophet that is relatable. He was just an average joe that God called anyway. He was a sheep breeder and a tender of sycamore fruit. He was a business man in many ways, but the Lord called him when he was minding his own business. Becoming a prophet was the last thing on Amos' mind. He had no professional training or theological education. There were no other prophets in his family but the Lord told him one day to go prophesy in an unfamiliar place called Bethel. In this place, is where he was mocked and asked not to prophesy again. In summary, God calls prophets in different ways.

Prophetic Exercise: Pray and ask the Holy Spirit to give you revelation of something that you had no knowledge of prior. Once you receive the revelation ask the Holy Spirit for the interpretation.

Quick Review:

1) What are some ways God calls a prophet?

2) Why does God deal with the mouth of a prophet when he calls them?

3) What must prophets do when they receive the call of a prophet?

4) Critical Thinking Question: What do you think would happen if someone refuses the call as a prophet?

CHAPTER FOURTEEN

Benefits Of Prophecy

There are so many benefits of prophecy. The religious folks will tell you that it's not relevant. I heard people say that there are no prophets and that Apostle Paul was the last apostle. This is pure ignorance and erroneous doctrine. If the teacher, pastor, and evangelist are still present, then why not the other two offices of the fivefold mentioned in Ephesians 4:1? Why is there such an attack against these two offices, the prophetic and the apostolic? The answer is that the devil doesn't want the people of God to come unto the full realization of the prophetic benefits.

> Ezekiel 37:1-4 (KJV) The hand of the Lord was upon me, and carried me out in the spirit of the Lord, and set me down in the

midst of the valley which was full of bones, And caused me to pass by them round about: and, behold, there were very many in the open valley; and, lo, they were very dry. And he said unto me, Son of man, can these bones live? And I answered, O Lord God, thou knowest. Again he said unto me, Prophesy upon these bones, and say unto them, O ye dry bones, hear the word of the Lord.

The first benefit of prophecy is that it brings life. In the passage above, prophecy brought life to the valley of dry bones. God was with the prophet Ezekiel and his spirit lead him to a dry place, wilderness, or desert land. Think about the prophetic training that you or most prophets had to endure. The desert place is where you learn how to prophesy. The dry place is where you get to see your prophetic words bring life to your dead situations. Once I owed thousands of dollars in restitution; in the natural there was no way for me to pay it off. I prayed and received instructions from God. I spoke and prophesied over my situation for months and then one day before the deadline of when the money was due, I was able to pay it off in full. Prophecy brings life! A prophetic word is so encouraging to people when they feel hopeless. The prophetic word gives them strength and renews their faith to continue on.

Prophecy gives spiritual vision. When it seems like everything around you is chaotic and going astray, the prophetic word can shed light on dark situations. Proverbs 29:13 says, "The poor and the deceitful man meet together: the Lord lighteneth both their eyes." God's word can cause you to look through the eyes of faith despite your faith being tested. When prophecy goes forth, you will begin to change your perspective on things. The prophetic word can bring revelation and causes someone to walk by blind faith. Blind faith is just simply allowing God to lead you and guide you. When God spoke to Abraham, he left everything behind (Genesis 12). A prophetic word can show you new things that God wants to do in your life. Isaiah 43:18-19 says, "Remember ye not the former things, neither consider the things of old. Behold, I will do a new thing; now it shall spring forth; shall ye not know it? I will even make a way in the wilderness, and rivers in the desert."

Proverbs 29:18 says, "Where there is no vision, the people perish: but he that keepeth the law, happy is he." Let's look at this scripture in the expanded bible. Proverbs 29:18 (EXB) says, " Where there is no ·word from God [vision; prophecy], ·people are uncontrolled [the people perish], but those who ·obey what they have been taught [guard the law] are happy [blessed]." As you go through trials in life, it is the prophetic word that gives you a vision to continue to do the work that you are called to do. Whenever you do new things or obey God and step out, there will be opposition. However, the prophetic word brings purpose, strength, and joy. You will begin to feel faith rise up in the inside and fight through all demonic resistance.

1 Corinthians 14:3 says, "But he that prophesieth speaketh unto men to edification, and exhortation, and comfort." Prophecy edifies, exhorts, and comforts. We have already discussed these three things in detail in the beginning of this book so let's move forward. Prophecy triggers other moves of the spirit of God. Prophecy allows the spontaneous flow of the

Holy Spirit to be present. When the Holy Spirit is flowing, the usual church programs will not work. God's spirit will move in a prophetic environment where all the needs in the house are met, people are healed and delivered. When prophecy is present, people don't leave the church the same way they came into the service. Acts 2:16-18 says, "But this is that which was spoken by the prophet Joel; And it shall come to pass in the last days, saith God, I will pour out of my Spirit upon all flesh: and your sons and your daughters shall prophesy, and your young men shall see visions, and your old men shall dream dreams: And on my servants and on my handmaidens I will pour out in those days of my Spirit; and they shall prophesy:"

Prophecy brings revival and restoration. When King Josiah was reigned he walked up rightly before God and he destroyed all the high places, idols, and began to rebuild the temple of the Lord. He tore his clothes when he discovered what the law had said that was found in the temple. He inquired of the Lord and his prophetess spoke a powerful word that brought forth change. The prophetic word spoken by Prophetess Huldah brought forth restoration and revival. Josiah called for the people to celebrate Passover and the ways of the Lord were remembered temporarily until a wicked King got back on the throne and established the idols (2 Kings 22-23).

Acts 13:1-3 says, "Now there were in the church that was at Antioch certain prophets and teachers; as Barnabas, and Simeon that was called Niger, and Lucius of Cyrene, and Manaen, which had been brought up with Herod the tetrarch, and Saul. As they ministered to the Lord, and fasted, the Holy Ghost said,

Separate me Barnabas and Saul for the work whereunto I have called them. And when they had fasted and prayed, and laid their hands on them, they sent them away." After everyone fasted and prayed, the prophetic word came forth and the people knew what God wanted them to do. Prophecy guides you to your right position in Christ. Prophecy is used by God to direct you where you need to go.

Prophetic Exercise: Pray and ask the Holy Spirit to give you five things to pray for. Be open to receive names, countries, and whatever else he gives you.

Quick Review:

1)   What are some benefits of prophecy?

2)   Why are the benefits of prophecy important?

3)   Why do you think there is such an attack on the prophetic?

4)   Critical Thinking Question: Can you think of any other benefits of prophecy that weren't discussed?

CHAPTER FIFTEEN

Preparation Of A Prophet.

Prophets have to go through a lot. Some people might think that becoming a prophet happens overnight, however that's simply not true. Some people may tell you that it takes about twenty years to become a prophet. In my opinion, it takes a lifetime to become a prophet because they are constantly evolving and embracing the things that God wants to do through them. Just when you think you've mastered something, God spontaneously does something new. When this occurs, you may feel as if you don't know what you are doing. The beautiful thing is that we allow the Holy Spirit to guide us and teach us. A person may be in prophetic office, but they still are being cultivated by the Father's hands. So, prophets have to go through intense training that occurs over a lifetime. Everything that you have been through in life from childhood to adulthood has prepared you to walk in your call as a prophet. Think about all the rejection that you have ever faced. The rejection that you experienced just prepared you to handle rejection better as a prophet. Think about all the lonely times you endured way before you ever discovered that you were a prophet. Well, the life of a prophet is a very lonely one.

God wants his prophets to die to themselves or kill their flesh. Before I saw the vision of Jesus Christ being crucified on the cross, I kept seeing myself in a casket. I was afraid of what I was seeing and I thought I was about to die. However, this was not the case. God was showing me that I was dying to myself. After the vision of Jesus on the cross, I received revelation and everything came together for me. I received the scripture Galatian 2:20 from the Holy Spirit and I started to feel the fire of God as never before. Galatians 2:20 says, "I am crucified with Christ: nevertheless I live; yet not I, but Christ liveth in me: and the life which I now live in the flesh I live by the faith of the Son of God, who loved me, and gave himself for me."

Luke 9:23 says, "And he said to them all, If any man will come after me, let him deny himself, and take up his cross daily, and follow me." As prophets, we need to deny ourselves and follow hard after Jesus. Our main goal as a prophet is to lift Jesus higher and not ourselves. We need to be about God's business and place our business on the back burner. This is a part of denying oneself. For instance, you might love the sunny land of California but God is calling you to the cold land of Alaska to do a great work for him so you have to go. A prophet has to be willing to go and allow God to lead them and submit fully to his plan. There were so many times when I wanted leave the state of Colorado but I knew that I couldn't because I was doing a great work where I was planted. I knew that as I yielded unto the Lord that one day He would give me my heart's desires.

When you are called as a prophet, you have to pay the price. You can't say, "Lord, I will follow you but first let me do this first." Let's look at the following passages:

Luke 9:59-62 says, "And he said unto another, Follow me. But he said, Lord, suffer me first to go and bury my father. Jesus said unto him, Let the dead bury their dead: but go thou and preach the kingdom of God. And another also said, Lord, I will follow thee; but let me first go bid them farewell, which are at home at my house. And Jesus said unto him, No man, having put his hand to the plough, and looking back, is fit for the kingdom of God."

At first it may seem as Jesus was cold-hearted, but that is not the case. He was telling the person if they want to come follow him, to not look back. You can't look back as a prophet of God. You can't spend too much time reflecting on the past and becoming stagnant on your journey with God. God has a new plan and purpose for your life as his prophet. As his prophet, you have nations to speak to; leaders to save; people to intercede for; projects to fulfill; and messages to deliver.

You can't be effective in your prophetic ministry by doing everything the world is doing. You can't be living a double life where you are portraying publicly to be a prophet but in private you are committing sexual immorality and doing things that grieve the spirit of God. Galatians 5:24 says, "And they that are Christ's have crucified the flesh with the affections and lusts." Prophets belong to Christ. They don't belong to themselves. Once, I had sinned against my own body and I could literally feel the distance between me and God. I didn't pray to God that night because I felt unclean and I thought maybe I could hide from him. God woke me up in the middle of the night. His presence was so strong in my room. I heard the external voice of God. It was loud like thunder. He spoke and said, "It's not about you." Immediately I got scared and I repented and I never committed sexual sin with my own self ever again.

Sometimes as a prophet, you will lose everything for a season. Abraham walked away from everything to pursue God (Genesis 12). You might hit rock bottom for a season. Joseph was in prison for years before God elevated him to being second-in-command in Egypt (Genesis 39-41). Remember, as God's prophet, he will sustain you. God sent the ravens to feed Elijah. 1 Kings 17:6 says, "And the ravens brought him bread and flesh in the morning, and bread and flesh in the evening; and he drank of the brook." As I accepted the call as a prophet, I lost people who I thought were my friends but I found a friend in the Holy Spirit. You have to decide that no matter what happens in this journey that you will go all the way with God. You have to be willing to lose everything to gain Christ and the anointing. Whatever you lose for God, you will gain back much more. Mark 8:35 says, "For whosoever will save his life shall lose it; but whosoever shall lose his life for my sake and the gospel's, the same shall save it."

As a prophet, you can't be insecure. The root of jealousy is insecurity. Whenever you are insecure, you will find yourself being intimidated by others and envying the anointing on their lives. You have to recognize that your identity is in Jesus Christ. You are hidden in Christ. Colossians 3:3 says, "For ye are dead, and your life is hid with Christ in God." The enemy wants you to be insecure and not being confident in your prophetic gifting. When you are confident in your gift, you will not allow the devil to cause thoughts of doubts in your mind. You will speak confidently what God is impressing upon you to say. I always tell my students just to step out and allow God to fill their mouths. I tell them that the Holy Spirit is never wrong but always accurate. I encourage my students to spend time with God before they prophesy. When they have been with God then there is no way that they are prophesying from a fleshy place but from the Holy Spirit. The prophecy will not always make sense to you but it should make sense to the recipient.

As a prophet, you can't have a fear of men. Some people are hindered in the prophetic because they worry about being liked. They don't want to give words of rebuke or correction when God is leading them too. Whenever you are fearful then you will not operate in faith. It takes faith to prophesy. Romans 12:6 says, "Having then gifts differing according to the grace that is given to us, whether prophecy, let us prophesy according to the proportion of faith." Fear will cause you to block your blessings and also cause a blockage of the recipient's blessings. A person is so blessed by the prophetic word that they will receive. If you are too fearful to give the word then that blood will be on your hands. Proverbs 29:25 says, "The fear of man bringeth a snare: but whoso putteth his trust in the LORD shall be safe."

Prophets have to be taking through the progress to get the need for acceptance out. Whenever you feel like you need to fit in, you might start compromising your walk with God. You will begin to idolize men and please them over God. As prophets, we have to be God-pleasers and not people-pleasers. There are many tribes and cliques in the body of Christ that go too far and cause division. These tribes and cliques think if they aren't with us then they are against us and that's wrong. 1 Corinthians 12:20 says, "But now are they many members, yet but one body." We are all a part of the body of Christ and we all have an assignment. Sometimes people will not fit in no matter how hard they try. I never fit in with the crowd. It seemed as no one liked me and I felt very alone at times. However, if God is for me who can be against me (Romans 8:31)? This is why it's so vital to not worry about people liking you. People will hate you when you are in the world and they will hate you even more when you are on fire for God.

Some prophets are birthed in the wilderness. This is my story. I am very non-traditional. God had to get me away from religious leaders and raise me up himself. I don't have any other prophets in my family nor did I receive any prophetic training at a biblical institution just like the prophet Amos when he was called. I was so stubborn that I ran from God and I had to get in a place where I could no longer run but to submit. I was like Jonah for a season. I am not against following church protocol but God deals with everyone differently. Some people's gifts can't be cultivated in a religious setting where the leader is holding them back or doesn't recognize the call on that person's life.

So, you might be thinking what is the wilderness? I have a CD on my store on my website going into detail about the wilderness. It's called, "Birthing Prophets in The Wilderness." The wilderness is an uncultivated, uninhabited, or inhospitable region. It is a dry, barren, rocky, broken land. It is also a dangerous, parched, dark land. This is a land where no one travels or passes through or lives. It is often described as a desert land or land of pits. Colorado was my wilderness.

Let's see what the bible says about the wilderness. Jeremiah 2:6 says, "Neither said they, Where is the Lord that brought us up out of the land of Egypt, that led us through the wilderness, through a land of deserts and of pits, through a land of drought, and of the shadow of death, through a land that no man passed through, and where no man dwelt?" Here's another verse. Jeremiah 50:12 says, "Your mother shall be sore confounded; she that bare you shall be ashamed: behold, the hindermost of the nations shall be a wilderness, a dry land, and a desert." The wilderness is not described as a comfortable place. The wilderness is a land of training. The wilderness is where you get to know God on a deeper level of intimacy. Now let's look at some prophets who got prepared in the wilderness.

Moses was in the wilderness for forty years. Numbers 32:13 says, "And the LORD'S anger was kindled against Israel, and he made them wander in the wilderness forty years, until all the generation, that had done evil in the sight of the LORD, was consumed." God did a great work through Moses in the wilderness and eventually raised him up to be a deliverer for His people. Moses was immature and had an anger issue until he went through the wilderness experience. Moses killed an Egyptian who was beating a Hebrew. He hid him in the sand. The next day, he saw two Hebrews fighting and one of them replied, "Are you going to kill me like you did the Egyptian." Moses fled into the wilderness and the Pharaoh found out that he killed the Egyptian. Moses went to a dry land called Midian. (Exodus 2).

One day, Moses was leading the flock back to the desert. He was on Mount Horeb where He had a supernatural encounter. God spoke to Moses from the burning bush, but the bush was not burned. God called his name and gave him his assignment. He was called to be a deliverer and bring the children of Israel out of Egypt. (Exodus 3). Moses did not find out who he was in God until he got into the wilderness.

Abraham had to go to a desert land. He went to Egypt. He had to leave everything and follow God to obtain the promises. Genesis 12:1-3 (KJV) says, "Now the Lord had said unto Abram, Get thee out of thy country, and from thy kindred, and from thy father's house, unto a land that I will shew thee: And I will make of thee a great nation, and I will bless thee, and make thy name great; and thou shalt be a blessing: And I will bless them that bless thee, and curse him that curseth thee: and in thee shall all families of the earth be blessed."

John The Baptist was a wilderness prophet. He was a forerunner. He was used to prepare the way for the Messiah. He did a great work for the Lord. God will use you in the wilderness. Matthew 3:3 (KJV) says, "For this is he that was spoken of by the prophet Esaias, saying, The voice of one crying in the wilderness, Prepare ye the way of the Lord, make his paths straight." In summary, God prepares his prophets through various life experiences and sometimes a wilderness experience.

Prophetic Exercise: Pray and ask the Holy Spirit to give you a prophetic song. This exercise will help you learn how to sing prophetically.

Quick Review:

1) How is someone prepared to be a prophet?

2) How important is it for prophets to go through the preparation process?

3) Give some bible examples of prophets who went through the preparation process.4) Critical Thinking Question: What process(es) have you or currently going through to become a prophet?

CHAPTER SIXTEEN

False Prophet

So many people are deceived and can't recognize a true prophet of God from a false prophet. They feel people are false prophets if they ask for money which is not necessarily the case when it takes money to finance the kingdom and its part of the biblical principles (1 Timothy 5:18, 1 Corinthians 9:11, 1 Samuel 9:7). We will discuss money and prophets later in this chapter. Some people feel like some prophets are false because they don't like them or don't agree with things in their ministry. This is not the case; I always tell my students to examine the fruit and stick with the scriptures. We will discuss the fruit of the Holy Spirit and the devil's fruit later in this chapter as well. For instance, there was a so-called prophet that I encountered on social media. He went around calling everyone a false prophet because he didn't like them, or if they challenged him then he would call them false. This was wrong. This so-called prophet caused a lot of division in the body of Christ. Once this prophet pronounced death on three apostles because they challenged him and exposed his malicious ways. The man said, "If I be a prophet of God, in three days you three will be dead." Well, his words fell to the ground and no death touched these apostles. I am so glad that I took the time and will continue to study on the biblical prophets. I have learned prophetic behavior or how different prophets behaved, their characteristics, and the challenges they endured.

Just because someone says that they are a prophet does not mean that they are. They have to be proven, tested, and tried. They have to be God-sent and not self-sent. They have to have the Holy Spirit and not any other kind of spirit. Most people that are prophets didn't originally want to become prophets, but later yielded to the call that's upon their lives. The bible warns us not to trust and believe every spirit. Just as the God of Abraham, Isaac, and Jacob has his prophets so does the devil (Revelation 2:20). 1 John 4:1 says, "Beloved, believe not every spirit, but try the spirits whether they are of God: because many false prophets are gone out into the world." Once, I met a self-called Apostle. He was false because he lacked the character of Christ. He was committing adultery, causing strife between different ministers, and he was a compulsive liar. I tried to be his friend and extend the gift of mercy, but the Holy Spirit inside of me was grieved so I had to cut off that relationship. The amazing thing was that as soon as I cut this man out of my life major doors opened for me. In a couple of days, television and international radio opportunities opened for me. Whenever you obey God, the blessings follow. I talk a lot about this in my book,

"Obedience Is Key." You have to pray for some people and move on in life. Not everyone is meant to be in your life and inner circle. Some people have hidden agendas and assignments from hell to destroy your life.

2 Corinthians 11:13-15 says, "For such are false apostles, deceitful workers, transforming themselves into the apostles of Christ. And no marvel; for Satan himself is transformed into an angel of light. Therefore it is no great thing if his ministers also be transformed as the ministers of righteousness; whose end shall be according to their works." As stated earlier, the devil has his prophets. They have hidden agendas against true prophets of God. The enemy's workers can pretend to be holy but denying the power of God. 2 Timothy 3:5 says, "Having a form of godliness, but denying the power thereof: from such turn away." The devil can prophesy (Acts 16:16-18) and he can do miracles (Exodus 7:20-22). I always tell my students not to get caught up in the gifts but examine the fruit and see if they have any Christ-like characteristics.

All throughout the prophetic books of the bible, we can see where the prophets had to prophesy against false prophets, wicked leaders, sinful people and nations. Jeremiah 23:25 says, "I have heard what the prophets said, that prophesy lies in my name, saying, I have dreamed, I have dreamed." False prophets lie and speak what God is not saying. For instance, when God is saying He will pronounce Judgment, it is the false prophets that speak that there will be peace in the land. This occurred in Jeremiah 14:13-14. The false prophets in Jeremiah's day were speaking the opposite of what God was really speaking.

As prophets, you have to make sure that you are really hearing from God. If God is not speaking then the best thing for you to do is to be quiet. Don't allow anyone to pressure you to speak what they want you to speak. You should only speak what God is telling you to speak. People have gotten upset with me because I didn't prophesy them a house or husband, but gave them a word of correction and a word about their spiritual condition.

The enemy's job is to deceive God's people. One of the devil's names is deceiver. Matthew 24:4-5 says, "And Jesus answered and said unto them, Take heed that no man deceive you. For many shall come in my name, saying, I am Christ; and shall deceive many." As children of God we have to constantly pray that the Lord increase our discernment so we can be sensitive to the Holy Spirit and be able to recognize spirits that are not of God. Many people have titles such as Prophet or Apostle in front of their names but no anointing to match. We have to be cautious of self-appointed social media prophets. You may be asking, "What's a self-appointed social media prophet?" These are the prophets that have no accountability, they prophesy all day on social media and their words may not have come from God; they have called themselves. I am not against social media, as it has been a blessing to my ministry. However, social media makes it easy to become something that you are not. On social media, you can portray that you are rich, successful, and good-looking by creating an alias when in reality you might be none of those things. Everything God tells you is not meant to be released. If you are truly spending time with God then you won't have time to be posting every 5 minutes on social media. Beware of those people that always claim that they have a word. I have to lay prostrate and wait on God for a while before I get words sometimes.

The first sign of a false prophet is that they preach a different gospel. 2 Peter 2:1 says, "But there were false prophets also among the people, even as there shall be false teachers among you, who privily shall bring in damnable heresies, even denying the Lord that bought them, and bring upon themselves swift destruction." Just like there are false prophets, there are false teachers, evangelists, pastors, and apostles. A true prophet of God would never preach anything contrary to God's word. A true prophet of God would never deny Jesus or be ashamed of him. A true prophet of God lifts Jesus higher, not themselves. A false prophet will preach things that sound good but twist the word of God. There was an incident that occurred a few years ago where this false prophet said that he was the Messiah and convinced everyone under his leadership to kill themselves. This is an example of damnable heresies. I tell my students to study the word of God for themselves. I have heard leaders preach things that weren't scriptural so as a teacher, I always teach from the word and not from some fleshy so-called revelation.

You may be wondering what is the best way to tell a false prophet from a true prophet. The answer is to test the fruits. Matthew 7:15-16 says, "Beware of false prophets, which come to you in sheep's clothing, but inwardly they are ravening wolves. Ye shall know them by their fruits. Do men gather grapes of thorns, or figs of thistles?" I stated earlier to be a fruit examiner. Just because you don't like someone doesn't make them false. That's just pure ignorance. It is our job as prophets to have a strong foundation of God's word inside of our hearts. Let's discuss the devil's fruit and the fruit of the Holy Spirit in order to bring clarity. Remember that a true prophet of God will have the fruit of the Holy Spirit.

The following scriptures discusses the devil's fruit. 2 Timothy 3:1-7 says, "This know also, that in the last days perilous times shall come. For men shall be lovers of their own selves, covetous, boasters, proud, blasphemers, disobedient to parents, unthankful, unholy, without natural affection, trucebreakers, false accusers, incontinent, fierce, despisers of those that are good, Traitors, heady, high-minded, lovers of pleasure more than lovers of God; Having a form of godliness, but denying the power thereof: from such turn away. For of this sort are they which creep into houses, and lead captive silly women laden with sins, led away with diverse lusts, Ever learning, and never able to come to the knowledge of the truth."

False prophets love money more than they love God. They are proud which God hates a proud look. False prophets speak lies, evil, and blasphemy the Holy Ghost. False prophets don't live Holy. False prophets disrespect elders and don't follow biblical principles of submitting and honoring their parents and leadership. False prophets are full of hate and don't show the love of God. False prophets carry unforgiveness and avenge themselves. They gossip and cause division. They lack self-control and they are involved in all sort of ungodly behavior. They lack compassion and empathy. They call evil good and good evil. They are full of betrayal and very impulsive. They are conceited and love the things of the world more than the things of God. They pretend to be righteous in public but in private they practice unrighteousness. They want to be God and deny the true power of God.

Now that we have discussed the devil's fruit or the things of the flesh, let's talk about good fruit. The good fruit is the fruit of the Holy Spirit and it's everything that Jesus stands for. Galatians 5:22-23 says, "But the fruit of the Spirit is love, joy, peace, longsuffering, gentleness, goodness, faith, Meekness, temperance: against such there is no law." True prophets of God show the love of God. They are peace makers. They know that the joy of the Lord is their strength. They are patient and gentle in spirit. They are full of faith and very meek. They have self-control and desire God more than the things of their flesh. As a prophet, you may not start off showing these fruits however if you go through the process that God wants to take you through and allow him to prune you then you will produce these fruits. You will become more like Christ and your old self will be unrecognizable. John 15:2 says, "Every branch in me that beareth not fruit he taketh away: and every branch that beareth fruit, he purgeth it, that it may bring forth more fruit."

Another way to recognize a false prophet is that their prophecies don't come to pass. Now, prophecies don't come to pass if it came from the prophet's flesh and God didn't speak it. Sometimes a budding prophet will speak presumptuously or boldly without authorization. In other words, God didn't release that prophet to speak those words or the prophet is illegal in the spirit which means that God will not back them up. Deuteronomy 18:21-22 says, "And if thou say in thine heart, How shall we know the word which the Lord hath not spoken? When a prophet speaketh in the name of the Lord, if the thing follow not, nor come to pass, that is the thing which the Lord hath not spoken, but the prophet hath spoken it presumptuously: thou shalt not be afraid of him." Samuel was a powerful prophet where none of his words fell to the ground which means that all his prophecies came to pass (1 Samuel 3:19). There were a few instances where some of the biblical prophet's words didn't come to pass. This is because God changed his mind. Jonah's prophecy of judgment on Nineveh didn't come to pass because the people repented and God is so merciful and he doesn't want anyone to perish. Jonah wasn't a false prophet but an immature one. To develop prophetic maturity, you have to go through the process that God wants to take you through. Only he knows how to break you and get things such as stubbornness, pride, rebellion, and other ungodly characteristics out of you.

False prophets lead you away from Jesus. Deuteronomy 13:1-4 says, "If there arise among you a prophet, or a dreamer of dreams, and giveth thee a sign or a wonder, And the sign or the wonder come to pass, whereof he spake unto thee, saying, Let us go after other gods, which thou hast not known, and let us serve them; Thou shalt not hearken unto the words of that prophet, or that dreamer of dreams: for the Lord your God proveth you, to know whether ye love the Lord your God with all your heart and with all your soul. Ye shall walk after the Lord your God, and fear him, and keep his commandments, and obey his voice, and ye shall serve him, and cleave unto him." False prophets want to be worshipped. They are self-centered and not God centered. They may even operate in signs and wonders. Remember the devil is a copycat and he doesn't do anything original. We have already discussed how Pharaoh's magicians were able to copy off Moses and Aaron in an earlier chapter. If someone calls themselves a prophet and operates in miracles but serves another God other than Jesus, then run.

False prophets live an unholy lifestyle. Jeremiah 23:14-15 says, "I have seen also in the prophets of Jerusalem an horrible thing: they commit adultery, and walk in lies: they strengthen also the hands of evildoers, that none doth return from his wickedness; they are all of them unto me as Sodom, and the inhabitants thereof as Gomorrah. Therefore thus saith the Lord of hosts concerning the prophets; Behold, I will feed them with wormwood, and make them drink the water of gall: for from the prophets of Jerusalem is profaneness gone forth into all the land." They do things that God calls an abomination (Proverbs 6:16). False prophets are dark and don't have the light of Christ within them. These are the prophets that will prophesy to you and sleep with you afterwards. They will speak seducing words just to control and manipulate you.

False prophets are money hungry. Instead of serving the God of Abraham, Isaac, and Jacob they serve the god of mammon or the god of money. They only preach and prophesy for money. They won't minister unless they get paid first. Their messages are mostly about money. They could care less about a person's spiritual condition. They are full of greed. Jeremiah 8:10-11 says, "Therefore will I give their wives unto others, and their fields to them that shall inherit them: for every one from the least even unto the greatest is given to covetousness, from the prophet even unto the priest every one dealeth falsely. For they have healed the hurt of the daughter of my people slightly, saying, Peace, peace; when there is no peace." A lady confiding in me once told me that this lady who calls herself an apostle got ten thousand dollars out of her. The apostle said to her, "God said if you sow $200 right now then your husband will come back home in two weeks." The lady was broken and desperate. Her husband was committing adultery and living with another woman. So, she did want the so-called apostle spoke. The lady's husband never came back home. The lady just kept sowing until she realized that she had sown about ten thousand dollars and none of those prophecies had come to pass. The so-called apostle lied on God and manipulated this hurting woman. This is a sign of false prophet and false apostle. They don't care about you; they only see you as a dollar sign.

False prophets only preach positive messages. Be aware if you never hear a prophet preach on sin or give words of rebuke. They don't want you to repent but they want you to get further in sin so they can profit off you (Hosea 4:8). When you look at the prophetic books in the bible, they all have something in common. The prophecies were balanced. The prophets spoke judgment, but also spoke of restoration. A false prophet will tell you that you are going to get blessed when you know you are deep in sin. They won't even prophesy against the sin or lead you back unto God. Jeremiah 23:16-17 says, "Thus saith the Lord of hosts, Hearken not unto the words of the prophets that prophesy unto you: they make you vain: they speak a vision of their own heart, and not out of the mouth of the Lord. They say still unto them that despise me, The Lord hath said, Ye shall have peace; and they say unto every one that walketh after the imagination of his own heart, No evil shall come upon you." False prophets are speaking out of their own spirit or heart and not speaking what God has spoken. They are speaking the opposite of what God is saying.

Prophetic Exercise: Pray and ask the Holy Spirit to give you a word of confirmation for someone. You can choose someone from your church, community, or on social media. Many times, the Lord will use you to speak words of confirmation and sometimes he will use you to prophesy new things. This exercise will help you build up the confidence to prophesy.

Quick Review:

1)   What is a false prophet?

2)   What are some characteristics of a true prophet of God?

3)   What are some characteristics of a false prophet?

4)   Critical Thinking Question: How can you discern a true prophet from a false prophet?

CHAPTER SEVENTEEN

Warfare

This chapter we will discuss various ways biblical prophets encounter warfare or conflicts. Prophets are predestined to go through warfare. Warfare is considered demonic attacks or opposition. It's when there is a lot of conflict surrounding the assignment that God has for you. Whenever you are doing something great for God, prepare for spiritual attacks. Whenever you have an assignment from God, prepare for spiritual resistance. Whenever you release a word you might get attacked from the spirit of backlash. Why must we go through warfare? Why does the enemy fight us so hard? The answer is to make us quit, to doubt God, and not fulfill our purpose. We can see this occur in the book of Nehemiah. He faced so much opposition trying to rebuilt the wall in Jerusalem (Nehemiah 4:1,7-8). Sanballat, Tobiah, the Arabians, the Ammonites, and the Ashdodites tormented and mocked Jews and Nehemiah. However, God gave him a strategy and they carried weapons so they can finish building (Nehemiah 4:17).

When I first started out in ministry, I was facing all kinds of challenges. I was being attacked financially and emotionally. It may seem that most ministers have to go through a season of lack or drought. God may give you a word about starting a business or a new project. In the natural you may think it's impossible because there is no money to get it completed. This is exactly what I went through. It seemed like every time I would accomplish something small then something major would happen to get me distracted or off course. For instance, I had paid off some expenses, then something happened with my car or something unforeseen happened and it costed a lot more money. I had to pray and fast and break those demonic attacks off my finances so I could prosper and get the work done for the Lord that he wanted me to do.

There were times when I was so rejected that it placed me into a deep state of depression. I withdrew myself from everyone. I just felt like being left alone and sleeping my life away. I could barely pray during that time, but I had to press my way through it. When this happens from time to time, I say, " I am going back into my cave." This statement comes from the story of Obadiah who was Ahab's steward. He put his life on the line to protect the prophets. He hid 100 prophets, 50 in each cave and he feed them bread and water because Jezebel was massacring the prophets of God (1 Kings 18:4).

The prophet Micaiah was attacked because he gave a word and the King didn't like it. King Ahab wanted to see if King Jehoshaphat would help him go to war against King Syria. Jehoshaphat wanted to inquire of the Lord first so Ahab called about four hundred prophets and asked them, "Should I go to war?" All the prophets replied, "Yes King Ahab because you will surely win the battle." King Jehoshaphat was skeptical because all the prophets were speaking the same thing so he asked if there was another prophet. King Ahab said, "Yes and I hate him because he never says anything nice." Well there was a lying spirit in the mouths of the prophets and Micaiah said the same thing as the other prophets. Eventually he gave the real word of the Lord. Micaiah said, "If you go to war then Ahab would die." At that instance, Zedekiah son of Kenaanah came up and slapped Micaiah and he was placed in prison. It is not certain if he ever got out because Ahab said, "Leave him there until I return safely." Well King Ahab died in war just as Micaiah had prophesied (1 Kings 22). Can you imagine being hated as a prophet? Can you imagine being put in prison for prophesying? This is the warfare Micaiah encountered for being obedient to his call as a prophet.

Elijah the mighty prophet of God who prayed down fire from heaven and killed the prophets of Baal in chapter 18. Elijah was a confrontational prophet. He was discouraged because Jezebel threatened his life (1 Kings 19). He became so discouraged that he fled and prayed to die. The Jezebel spirit isn't gender-specific, but it's one of the biggest enemies against the prophets. It seems that many prophets of today can have a spiritual high in God where the supernatural and miracles are flowing through them. Then shortly afterwards, they hit a spiritual low where they get so discouraged that they want to just quit and walk away from the call of God. Why do prophets have high highs and low lows? It's actually common among most prophets. The cure for this is to stay in God's presence, meditate on the word, prayed up, and focus on Jesus. All of these will help a prophet not to get in their emotions but stay walking by faith.

Jeremiah was a mighty prophet who is also known as a weeping prophet since he wrote the book of lamentations. He truly carried the burden of the Lord. The anointing on Jeremiah's life was confrontational just like Elijah. Both of these prophets were bold and spoke openly against sin. Since Jeremiah prophesied against Baal worship (Jeremiah 19) the people hated him and put his head in stocks (Jeremiah 19). He was about to be decapitated. However, it wasn't his time to go yet. God rescued him. God is sure to deliver his prophets and protect them when their assignment isn't complete. Psalm 105:15 says, "Saying, touch not mine anointed, and do my prophets no harm." God also sent someone to rescue Jeremiah when he was thrown in a well (Jeremiah 38:1-6). The people hated the word that he was delivering and they plotted against him. He could have died when he was thrown into the well. Yet the hand of the Lord was upon him. Jeremiah wanted to quit but he said, "Lord you are like fire shut up in my bones (Jeremiah 20:9)." He couldn't quit even if he wanted to. Prophets must have tenacity.

Most prophets have gotten attacked at birth. When I was a baby, I almost experienced crib death. One day, my mother screamed. She yelled, "Kimberly is not breathing!" Immediately my dad who was certified in CPR flipped me on my belly and did hard hits on my back until my air way cleared. I was full of phlegm. The enemy wanted to take me out as a baby. Moses was attacked at birth. The wicked pharaoh put a decree to throw all the male children in the Nile river (Exodus 1:12, 16, 22). However, Moses' parents hid him for a short amount of them and he was eventually raised by the pharaoh's daughter. Jesus was attacked at birth because the wicked King Herod got jealous. He heard someone say, "King of the Jews." The devil entered into King Herod and he had all the male children under the age of two in Bethlehem massacred (Matthew 2:2,13,16). An angel of the Lord appeared to Joseph and told him to take his family and flee to Egypt.

Prophetic Exercise: This is the ultimate test. This exercise will increase your prophetic flow. Pray and ask the Holy Spirit who you shall call. Once you call them, pray and prophesy over them for no less than five minutes. Make sure that you place your timer on before you start.

Quick Review:

1) Why do prophets go through warfare?

2) What are the kinds of warfare that prophets go through?

3) What can prophets do to not have so many high highs and low lows?

4) Critical Thinking Question: What way(s) have you been attacked by the enemy and how did you overcome it?

Curriculum

Here is the actual course schedule that I use for my school. The following curriculum is used for a monthly and a weekly schedule, or almost two months. For instance, teach during a certain time frame such as one hour and allow room for Q&A at the end to help stay on schedule.

You can even teach for almost three months by teaching two chapters out of this book per session. You can turn this schedule into almost four months by teaching one chapter per session. I highly recommend doing some prophetic activations after teaching each class so that the students are able to get some hands-on training.

Course Schedule

Class	Schedule
1	Is the school of the prophets biblical? Mentorship, What is Prophecy?
2	Hearing God's Voice, Lifestyle of a Prophet, The Spirit of Prophecy
3	The Gift of Prophecy, The Office of a Prophet, Gifts Of The Spirit.
4	Functions Of A Prophet, Call Of A Prophet, Benefits of Prophecy?
5	Preparation Of A Prophet, False Prophets, Warfare

About The Author

Kimberly Hargraves is a highly sought after prophetic voice, Intercessor and a prolific author. There is no doubt that she has a global mandate on her life to serve the nations of the world by spreading the Gospel of JesusChrist. She has a quickly expanding worldwide healing and deliveranceministry. Kimberly Hargraves wears many hats to fulfill the call God has placed on her life as an entrepreneur over several businesses including her own personal brand Rejoice Essentials which promotes the Gospel of Jesus Christ. This brand includes a magazine and anointing oils. She also serves as a life coach and mentor to many women. She is also the loving mother of two wonderful children. Kimberly has dedicated her life to the work of ministry and to serve others under the call God has placed over her life.

Kimberly currently resides in Colorado.She is a very anointed woman of God who signs, miracles and wonders follow. The miraculous and incessant testimonies attributed to her ministry are incalculable, with many reporting physical and mental healing, financial breakthroughs, debt cancellations and other favorable outcomes. She is known across the globe as a servant who truly labors on behalf of God's people through intercession. God blessed her to start her ministry to help encourage others. God used her pain to reveal her writing ability and to do his work. God blessed her to write about life experiences and give a message of hope to others with broken hearts.

She is the author of The Following:

"Overcoming Difficult Life Experiences with Scriptures and Prayers"

"Overcoming Emotions with Prayers"

"Daily Prayers That Bring Changes"

"In Right Standing,"

"Obedience Is Key,"

"Prayers That Break The Yoke Of The Enemy: A Book Of Declarations,"

"Prayers That Demolish Demonic Strongholds: A Book Of Declarations,"

"Work Smarter. Not Harder. A Book Of Declarations For The Workforce,"

"Set The Captives Free: A Book Of Deliverance."

"Pray More Challenge"

"Empowering The New Me: Fifty Tips To Becoming A Godly Woman"

You can find more about Kimberly at

www.kimberlyhargraves.com. Follow Kimberly on Facebook at https://www.facebook.com/seerprophetesskimberlyhargraves/.

Follow Kimberly on Twitter and periscope @SeerProphetessK.

Reference

1. God's Arithmetic. (n.d.) Retrieved April 9, 2017 from http://asis.com/users/stag/arithme.html

2. "What is the church?" (n.d.). Retrieved April 9, 2017 from https://www.gotquestions.org/what-is-the-church.html

3. THAYER'S GREEK LEXICON, Electronic Database. Copyright © 2002, 2003, 2006, 2011 by Biblesoft, Inc. All rights reserved. Used by permission. BibleSoft.com

4. Helps Word Studies copyright © 1987, 2011 by Helps Ministries, Inc. For complete text and additional resources visit: TheDiscoveryBible.com

5) Dr. Jimmie Reed Ministries. http://www.revelationinternational.org https://www.facebook.com/Revelation-International-Dr-Jimmie-Reed-540956312729400/?ref=nf

6) "Oracle." Merriam-Webster.com. Merriam-Webster, n.d. Web. 15 Apr. 2017.

7. "Celibacy." Merriam-Webster.com. Merriam-Webster, n.d. Web. 20 Apr. 2017.

8. "Admonition." Merriam-Webster.com. Merriam-Webster, n.d. Web. 23 Apr. 2017.

9. "Initiate." Merriam-Webster.com. Merriam-Webster, n.d. Web. 23 Apr. 2017.

10. "Theology." Merriam-Webster.com. Merriam-Webster, n.d. Web. 23 Apr. 2017.

Order Additional Copies At

www.republishing.org

Index

A

Abraham, 79, 83, 95, 101, 105, 108, 115
Agabus, 79
Ahab, 82, 120
Amaziah, 90
Amos, 9, 79, 90–91
Ananias, 64–65
angel, 38, 40, 55, 65, 75, 77, 85, 109, 122
angelic ministers, 22
anointing, 5, 11, 31, 53–54, 58, 61, 66, 73, 101–2, 110, 121
Apostle Paul, 13, 17, 61–62, 67–68, 79, 93
apostles, 31, 57, 60, 69, 108–11, 116
Asaph, 74
atmosphere, 37, 39, 42, 45
authority, 58, 62

B

Barnabas, 74, 96–97
basic level prophecy, 20
believers, 16–17, 25, 35, 58, 60, 65–66, 69, 75
benefits, 13, 63, 93–94, 97, 124
blessings, 32, 85, 102, 105, 108, 110
business, 58, 60, 91, 99, 119, 125

C

celibacy, 68, 127
Christ, Jesus, 50, 54–55, 60, 99, 102, 125
church, 11, 16–17, 19–20, 47–49, 57, 61, 69, 76, 81, 96, 117
class, 2–5, 42–43, 48–49, 123–24
comfort, 16–18, 26, 33, 47–48, 57, 87, 95
company of prophets, 7, 41–42
confirmation, 5, 58, 117
correction, 2, 47, 58, 77–78, 102, 110
counsel, 49, 72, 77
Critical Thinking Question, 9, 14, 21, 27, 36, 44, 52, 59, 70, 86, 92, 97, 106, 117, 122
crucifixion, 55–56

D

Daniel, 71–72, 77, 83, 85
David, 7, 39, 74, 76, 84
devil, 23, 31, 62–63, 81, 93, 102, 108–9, 115, 122
direction, 10, 58, 76
dreams, 53, 56, 76–77

E

edification, 16, 48, 57, 95
Eli, 13, 88
Elijah, 8, 26, 78, 82, 84, 101, 120–21
Elisha, 8, 33, 83–84
enemy, 22–23, 27, 32, 34–35, 39–40, 84, 90, 102, 120, 122, 126
evangelists, 31, 51, 57, 64, 93, 111

exhortation, 16–17, 47–48, 57, 68, 95
Ezekiel, 73, 78, 81–82, 93

F

false prophets, 18, 50, 72, 78, 81, 107–9, 111–17, 124
fasting, 22, 30–31, 39, 47, 74, 83
flesh, 18, 42, 56, 73, 75, 96, 99, 101, 113
fruits, 16, 107, 109, 111–13
  devil's, 107, 112–13
functions, 37, 71, 85–86, 124

G

Gad, 76, 84
gifts
  power, 63, 65
  vocal, 63, 66
gospel, 11–12, 60, 67, 101, 111, 125
guidance, 76

H

Habakkuk, 72, 75
healings, 11, 46, 62–63, 65–66, 69, 83, 125
Hearing God, 6, 22–23, 124
heart, 18–19, 23, 29–30, 39, 41, 47, 49, 58, 72–73, 78, 100, 112, 114, 116–17
heaven, 8, 33, 35, 56–57, 120
Hezekiah, 72, 74

Holy Ghost, 12, 18, 38–40, 62, 79, 96, 112
Hosea, 62, 78, 116

I

Isaiah, 72, 82, 84, 88–89, 95
Israel, 31, 38–39, 76, 78–79, 82, 84, 90, 104–5

J

Jeduthun, 75
Jeremiah, 23, 34, 72–74, 77, 82–83, 87–90, 104, 109, 115–16, 121
Jethro, 12
Jezebel, 82, 119–20
Jonah, 34, 81, 103, 114
judgment, 75, 78, 80–81, 88, 114, 116

K

knowledge, 36, 40, 46, 56, 62–65, 67, 85, 91, 112

L

leaders, 11, 14, 82, 84, 100, 104
love, 16–19, 32–33, 61, 99, 112–13

M

marriages, 15, 22, 63, 68

Mary, 38–39
mentor, 8, 10, 12–13, 125
mentorship, 7–8, 10, 13–14, 124
Messiah, 39, 75–76, 105, 111
Micah, 78, 82
Micaiah, 120
ministry, 8, 13, 32, 34, 51, 57–63, 66, 68–69, 71, 85, 107, 110, 119, 125, 127
miracles, 31–32, 62–63, 65, 69, 83, 109, 115, 120, 125
money, 94, 107, 115, 119
Moses, 12–13, 31, 80, 83, 85, 104–5, 115, 122

N

Nathan, 84
Nehemiah, 118–19

O

office, 7, 11, 37, 45–47, 53, 57–58, 60, 93, 124
oracles, 16, 32, 50–51, 89, 127

P

peace, 38, 40, 82, 109, 113, 116
persecution, 35, 73
Phillip, 51
praise, 17, 34, 50
prayer, 15, 17, 22–26, 29–31, 35–37, 46–47, 71–72, 83, 126
preach, 46, 58, 100, 111, 115–16

priest, 40, 84, 88, 116
promises, 24, 75–76, 105
prophecy, judge, 80–81
prophesying, 18–20, 23, 42, 47–48, 50, 52, 67, 71, 102, 120
prophet Elisha, 8, 33
prophetess, 5, 39, 54, 96
Prophetess Anna, 39
Prophetess Huldah, 96
prophetic, 2–3, 8, 15–20, 27, 33, 37, 47, 50–51, 93, 97, 102
prophetic anointing, 2, 42, 47, 54
prophetic atmosphere, 42, 44
prophetic flow, 20, 28, 49, 122
prophetic lifestyle, 2, 36
prophetic mantles, 42, 83
prophetic office, 5, 57, 98
prophetic training, 50, 94, 103
prophetic word, 16–17, 19, 73, 81, 94–97, 102
prophet Iddo, 84
prophet Joel, 43, 96
prophet Obadiah, 82
Prophet Samuel, 7, 42, 84

R

rejection, 26, 33, 71, 73, 99
revelatory gifts, 56, 63
righteousness, 2, 32, 40, 69, 109
root, 77, 90, 102

S

Samuel, 7, 13, 40–42, 73, 76, 83–84, 88, 107, 114
Saul, 7, 41–42, 65, 74, 96–97
secrets, 26, 29, 49, 79
seer, 74, 76–77, 84
seraphims, 88–89
spiritual gifts, 13, 18–19, 47, 58, 61–62, 68–70
strongholds, 77, 81

T

teachers, 2, 31, 57, 69, 93, 96, 111
temple, 13, 38–40, 88, 96
Timothy, 2–3, 13, 17, 73, 83, 107, 109, 112
tongues, 48–49, 52, 62–63, 65, 67, 69, 73
  interpretation of, 62–63, 67
tribes, 103

V

visions, 42–43, 53, 55–56, 76–77, 95–96, 99, 116
voice of God, 22–24, 26–27, 88

W

warfare, 54, 56, 71, 118, 122, 124
wilderness, 31, 34, 36, 85, 94–95, 103–6
wisdom, 7, 30, 56, 62–64, 69, 80
worship, 2, 17, 22, 25, 33–34, 37–38, 43, 47, 74

Z

www.ingramcontent.com/pod-product-compliance
Lightning Source LLC
Chambersburg PA
CBHW071735080526
44588CB00013B/2047